Whale Road

Whale Road

D.K. McCutchen

JACKLEG PRESS

JackLeg Press
www.jacklegpress.org

ISBN: 978-1956907018

Originally published by Vintage Books, Auckland, New Zealand,
2004. Second edition published by Blake Publishing, 2006.

Library of Congress Control Number: 2023933887

Cover image: *Rising Torments* by Reb Livingston

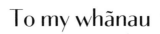

To my whãnau

Hwaelweg: The Path of the Whale. The Ocean.

—Joseph Bosworth & T. Northcote Toller's
Anglo Saxon Dictionary, 1921

Table of Contents

Prologue

Flying South

Everything I tell you is a lie.
—The Liar's Paradox

MY SHIPMATE SIMON FELL OFF Taiaroa Head, near the royal albatross colony on the South Island of New Zealand. The crumbling headland of the harbor is a high point of land topped by cropped grasses; green edges overhang bare yellow earth and rock that plummets straight down into the Great Southern Ocean. Simon was always accident-prone.

Young albatross use these cliffs as a jumping-off point, a slow glide into journeys that take them around all the oceans of the world. As juveniles, they don't land on the earth for up to two years after that initial tilt over the windy edge of their birthplace. There can be no practice flights to get it right. They spread four-meter wingspans out over the waves on the first try and never look back.

I met Simon in Tahiti. We had flown in from opposite ends of the world to join an expedition sailing through the South Pacific to New Zealand. The research vessel was following 'The Line' mapped by the old whalers hunting for sperm whales. The whalers' logs claimed whales were once so numerous and clustered along this path, it seemed they formed a black road. We were there to see if any whales were left at all.

Simon wrote faithfully in his journal for a few weeks, bemoaning his seasickness and the green New Zealand islands he had left behind, wondering what the future held, and finally writing only about the stark beauty of the endless waves. Then the entries became erratic, until he gave up writing altogether for sleeping whenever the chance arose. He gave me what writings he had, in a green cloth-bound journal much like my own, when we sailed months later into the Hauraki Gulf and the Waitemata Harbor, Auckland. Perhaps that is something active, accident-prone people do: they give their accountings to those of us who hoard and record. It showed his instinct, his talent, to shed and disperse all the clutter of life—even his past, a trait I think birds and sailors share.

Weeks after he flew from the cliffs, I rowed out to see adult albatross gyring overhead in the wind funnel over Taiaroa Head. Balancing in a wooden dinghy, looking up at the spot from which Simon fell, I could see a long scroll of golden tussock-grass overhanging the edge like swept hair, marking the one narrow section of cliff that was undercut, grooved out by the waves and supported on either side by huge flying buttresses of rock. It was the only place on the cliffs that dropped straight down into deep water. From below, the bluff became a grass-topped cathedral crowned by a circlet of winged creatures. From far away, their cries sounded like human voices calling: 'No-no. No. No.'

The ocean creates its voice from the clinking of sand and the pluck of rain, from the descant of whales and the mollusks' bellow. Simon, the bird- man, must have been glad enough of attaining the water's grace that night on the cliffs, when he made his virgin flight. He always was lucky.

Landing Upright

IT IS WINTER IN THE Northern Hemisphere. I stare out my library window. Instead of green pines in snow, I see only internal seas and a blazing sun. Simon's journal is in my hand with its spare, day-by-day account of the first days of our expedition, chasing whales across the ocean. I turn the scribbled pages and moments wash over me: the smells, the heat, the horror of seasickness for weeks without relief.

We were the newest members of the crew. Our bodies lay utterly immobilized in the brilliant heat, collapsed in the cockpit of a pitching sailboat. We began telling each other stories to keep the longing for land, our homes, at bay. Queasiness became the darkness from which all stories welled up like cool water. I can hear Simon's voice—that precise Auckland accent—as I read his journal. I envision snipping a few moments from my memories, from Simon's words—from invention—to give my daughter a glimpse of her own beginnings. I can feel her wriggling in my belly, bumping and head-butting, flipping end over end like the tadpoles one sees inside frogs' eggs before they hatch. I want to tell her about the journey that led to her.

My daughter basks in her amniotic ocean as I wait by my window. I fall easily into dreaming while sorting through these old papers, trying to imagine how I will raise this gift of a girl-child. I want to create some kind of predictable order out of a lifetime of chaos, reflected in the clutter of papers and journals on the desk.

My younger self had a restless imperative: to keep searching further afield, explore the world. The adventure is internal now. Change and no change. She shifts inside me, and a hollow uneasiness makes me hug the tattered book to my belly. Morning sickness. Past and present ebb and flow through a sea of voices.

1.
Northern Fall

Leaving Home

THEY BROUGHT OUT A BOOK with white pages, blank as the faces in a crowded room. Look, they said proudly, keep a record. Take us with you. Share. This is where it starts then, where the stories always start—with goodbyes.

I REMEMBER AUTUMN, NOT MAPLE-sugaring time in spring. Too early for apples. It must have been grapes. I will write it grapes.

What happens to a grape-stomper with athlete's foot, I ask, and they laugh and keep picking, fingers stained dusky purple and wine. The light dapples through the crisscrossed vines overhead, high fall sky bluing to black. Satisfying clumps of tiny purple, huge red and medium green hang just beyond the trellis, reaching up through, threading between vines. The ripest drop without plucking, softly roll down faces and necks, staining shirts, landing in the round bowls held on hips. A rain of plump, dusky fruit scatters at our feet. The triangular shapes of the clumps fit each hand and come away easily from the vine, then tangle in last-minute tendrils wound around yellowing leaves. The sky peeps through the cool leaves of the trellis, allowing only infrequent beams of light to touch the ground. Grapes squish to pale pulp underfoot; leaves rustle. The pickers let a few grapes roll into dry mouths, biting the tough skins and letting the elastic middles squeeze out tart and bitter and sweet. The leathery skins and seeds are spat out on the ground. The

1

brave chew them, too, for the texture: tart autumn grapes, sweetened by frost.

Baskets, bowls and buckets pile up for the press, wait for the grandmothers' hands to pluck from their tiny trellises, the cask of blue skin, taut with green flesh. Their grandson hasn't seen the pressing, wants to crawl under the barrel while his grandfather and auntie turn the press together, clear lavender juice pouring into the bowl. The boy sticks his hand in the sticky stream, unseen, licks his fingers and lets the tart liquid sluice down his arm onto the grass. He makes a face and puckers his mouth, tongue flicking like a cat's. More is better and his little fingers divert the stream again. I make him get his cup. His grandfather laughs and stirs the mash for another go. The three grandmothers giggle and keep plucking fruit from the twining fingers of the vine.

The yellow leaves are breathing. The yellow pile is pulsing with the breath of some small creature. A grandmother goes searching and sees the moving leaves; stops to smile and wonder aloud where her grandson can be. The leaves shake. She gently taps a stray curl of hair, caught up in the leaf stems, and the pile erupts into laughing little boy.

He buries me next—the auntie who is leaving soon—and we hide as the grandmother rakes the pile higher. She is called away to the grape press and we are left together in a yellow world, private and sunny. I blow some veined gold webs away from my mouth, and he begins to blow them all away from my face and hair. I pile more leaves on his head and we sit and breathe in the musk of an early autumn in our

2

rustling nest. He points to the high clouds and snuggles into my belly, naming his toy *blancheau* bear in the biggest, fattest puff of white. I am surprised that he is suddenly old enough to see things in other things. Clouds are no longer too far away to name. He captures a tiny red leaf, makes me a present of it, and we make a bouquet for the new baby, a brother or sister. He is the first. He is appalled, enthralled, that his auntie has a brother and a sister already. His daddy is my brother, and this makes him hesitate, thinking.

He likes the word *bouquet*, and we add a huge red leaf and one peach-colored with odd moles. He tells me these are, yes, part of the leaf. He does not like bugs. I do not tell him about the tiny spiders drifting on silk through the leaf pile with us. I sing him a song about brothers and sisters and wonder when I became so moral. He doesn't seem to balk at the idea of loving the bulge in his mummy's tum, the one that isn't turned the right way round and makes it hard for her to hug him. He tries to fit a leaf into my ear and asks if everyone has a baby inside, and I tell him no. My stomach is empty.

Life here has been this family, this farm, a sibling's child, and outside work that isn't my calling: sweating in one of the local hotshops as a glassblower's assistant. I'm trading rolling hills and hot glass for southern oceans and dreams. My family for someone else's. This moment for restless wandering.

We disappear again into veined yellow, peeking through a maze of leaves. Imagining what will happen when the rakes take all the gold to barrels, and the snow starts to fall on the still-green grass.

The Last Whale

THE GRANDMOTHERS TOLD A STORY before we sailed southward; one for the road. It had come to them from a northern fisherwoman, down East Maine, who'd had it from a Micmac elder. They told it on a sunny day from a hilltop farm, cicadas sizzling in the grass like water percolating down through a packed-sand beach.

A child-man of The People went to the beach of bones and saw the last whale. It was big and it was warm in the cold sea, and it called to him.

—Come on my back, hu-man. See what it is I see here in the deep world ocean.

So the man swam to find out. He swam to the wall-like side of the whale and climbed painfully up the ragged calluses on her head until he stood upright on her back. Then he sat upon the whale, and he lay upon the whale, and finally he hugged the whale as it pushed up towering, curled waves along each side of the massive head moving through the water's narrow surface. He reached his arms as far along her sides as he could and pressed his face into the whale. The whale's warm breath boiled up from her two blowholes and the man breathed the breath of the whale. It was oily and rich with a hungry memory, the fresh ozone smell of schooling herring. And it was good.

The whale dived down,

and down,

And still the hu-man breathed her breath and saw what the whale saw, and the sky became scattered tatters of hard glitter above them through the ceiling of the ocean.

Slowly deeper, quickly blacker, and the man, who saw with the whale's eyes, was blinded by a sudden, thick dark and he/she was afraid.

The great hearts beat together a sudden flutter and man and whale panicked for the thinner—the lighter—air and rose in a rushing gasp from the dark where not even squid lights glimmered past.

—What is it? What?

The man, borne again on the waves, learning to breathe on his own, again colder.

—What?

—What is it? cried the whale in quaking, rumbling terror that made the child-man throw his arms around her for comfort. And they huddled on the thin, flat surface of the world, all fragile, cold flesh to flesh, warm breaths misting widened eyes, and peered down through the reflecting glass of the water into the dark secret of their mother ocean.

And they saw nothing.

Nothing at all.

2.
Tahitian Heat: September

Leviathan, n. An enormous aquatic animal mentioned by Job. Some suppose it to have been the whale, but that distinguished ichthyologist, Dr. Jordon of Stanford University, maintains with considerable heat that it was a species of gigantic Tadpole (Thaddeus polandensis) or Polliwog-Maria Pseudo-hirsute. For an exhaustive description and history of the Tadpole consult the famous monograph of Jane Porter, Thaddeus of Warsaw.

—Ambrose Bierce,
The Devil's Dictionary

First Impressions

COLD, STUFFY PLANE AIR GASPING out into damp night-time heat. Sleepy welcome singers with wilted flower leis. A tired woman waiting, looking through each debarking passenger, unsure.

Driving silently along the waterfront in the dark of early morning, diesel smelling and jasmine, watching a tall brown girl walking, head high, a single red hibiscus flower blooming in her blue-black hair. The road along the waterfront, black tar; narrow, black sand beach crisscrossed with stiff hemp mooring lines; a tiny pale dinghy for too-large traveling bags. Water running down arms that pull the heavy lines overhead, moving the dinghy under and out towards sleeping yachts. Tahiti.

Blue-hulled yacht, too small, too dirty. Cloudy crayon marks on a teak deck, white plastic cockpit, half a body-length wide, scattered with square, orange cushions and chipped teacups, a legless highchair and tray table strapped to the rail beside odd instruments, jerry cans, pikes and nets. Down the ladder, backwards into dark, smell of old food, scattered crusts of bread underfoot. Clutter of cables and instruments under the single light over the chart table, the stale breath of sleeping bodies, white-sheeted figures in bunks and hammocks in a too-small space. The dim light glinting on one pair of eyes staring straight upwards into dark.

Curling, still dressed, on a rough cushion, blue-green tweed smelling sour, cheek pressed hard into the coarse weave. Lights off. Bodies breathing. The subliminal shift and stagger of a tethered boat in harbor.

The Boat People

THE RIDE FROM THE AIRPORT last night has thin brown hair pulled back so tightly the straight, wide part looks painful. Pretty, almond-colored eyes and a stubborn/ingratiating tuck to the chin.

The morning cup of tea in the galley wears crisp beige sailor shorts, tremendous round glasses under a fat Rasta hat, straight, silky nut-brown hair half the length of a short, neat body. Small, dark, and not at all pleased.

New blond ponytail up on deck, thick hair, not sun-yellowed yet. Enthusiastic, too nice, too young, too thin, bare tops of feet already burnt to blistering, tiny white stars on a sky of red meat. Relaxed as a cat against the rail, folded over a stubbed and bloody toe.

Two children stagger aft, sun-haired shy babies, taller red shorts with matching, red-circled eyes. Little bonnet's thin, bare legs spotted with purple sores, diaper sagging under an orange harness. Smiles for eye contact, soft touches and gentle leaning against a new knee, hoping for a pat, a story, some time.

Tall red mop of tangled curls, almost dreads, working on the sails mid-decks. Skin red and sloughing. Shapeless, shabby, forgettable shorts, long forgotten. Blue eyes shifting away like restless water.

Captain, Wife, Children, Mate, Deckhand; crewmates on a too-small boat.

Cockpit Confessions

THE BLOND PONYTAIL'S FIFTEEN MINUTES of fame were as the guy who got his hand stuck in the photocopying machine at the Wildlife Department back home. He was just trying to pull out a jammed paper and the hand got in there under the inkers and the rollers and the mashers, and he just wasn't going anywhere until the repairman showed up. The worst part, he said, was everyone trooping past the mailroom door to have a good wheeze at his expense. And then that same week he and his best mate, Temuera, had dumped the department's dinghy in the surf and lost all the good photography equipment overboard. Most people didn't know about that one, though.

Most horrifying moment? Oh, that was easy: that was when he was taking all the rubbish from his supervisors' lab to the tip. The tip? What do Americans call it? A dump? Anyway, he grabbed a black plastic bag sitting next to the front door and took the whole lot away. Got back to find his supervisors going mad trying to find the bag with the entire season's field work, all their undeveloped negatives of the whales in Kaikoura Bay. He spent the next two days picking through the pong of old rubbish, trying to find the films. No luck. He reckoned he'd never live that one down. A whole season's work. No wonder they wanted him to come on this sailing trip; he wouldn't be able to get up their noses for an entire season.

Girlfriend? Nuh, not really. Well, maybe one girl he liked, but he reckoned she wouldn't have him. He kept busy

12

back home working on a project concerning the tuatara—a not-quite-lizard with almost three eyes—with his school chums, and a seabird project with his mate, Temuera, and the local Maori *iwi*. He'd left everything on hold to come on this trip. It was a bit stressful, really: he owed money, and something was going on with his parents, not sure what; he'd find out when he got back. He was on his mum's side rather, but wished they'd work it out. Didn't believe in marriage himself. Just didn't work, did it? NO. No kids, thanks. Couldn't imagine it, actually. Bad enough the wee boy over there thought he was a punching bag in the early a.m. Little grub. He liked kids okay, just didn't want to add to the world's population problem, right?

Dreams? Oh, running a whale research project out of Tonga, he reckoned, or being some kind of negotiator between the scientists and the wildlife managers. He thought that would be it, really. Seemed those groups never talked, that someone who knew both sides and didn't have an agenda could be really useful in that kind of job. Right now, he just wanted the captain to ask him to go on with the boat, sail with them back to Canada—now that would be an adventure! Canada seemed pretty exotic. America just sounded scary, all those cities and car chases: dangerous, really. But Canada! That would be choice. And here he was, carked out on his back in the cockpit, barely able to keep his tea down when he sat up. No bloody good to anyone.

Favorite reading? Well . . . he was supposed to be reading his research papers right now, but it was hard to concentrate, not to mention sick-making. He reckoned

Terry Pratchett was good for a laugh. Yeah, 'course he'd read *Moby-Dick*, it was down in the main cabin. Well, no, he hadn't finished it either.

Most painful moment? Well, on his way here, he fell over, really bashed his elbow, worse than the sunburn, worse than stubbing his big toe bloody on the deck cleat the day he arrived. No, just walking down the street in Auckland. Didn't trip, no. Just fell over. No idea. Accident-prone? No, not really. He just fell over, didn't he? Everyone falls over now and then.

Whales? Bloody oh yeah. Whales were brilliant. He reckoned he knew most of the Kaikoura catalogue by heart—he'd put the thing together, after all. His supervisor said he knew more New Zealand whales by sight than anyone living. Wanted to see if he recognized any of them up here near the equator, if we ever found any. Bit frustrating really, knowing the expedition had been at sea for so long already without a whale to be heard. Couldn't go out a single day in Kaikoura without finding whales. And then he got to go back to his dry, non-rocking bed and a decent feed at night.

Why was he here? For the experience. Too right. His whole life was up in the air when he got home; who knew what would happen? Better not to think about it. And yes, it was pretty rough out here right now, but the captain was tops in cetacean research, the best. Course there were no whales, and the heat was brutal, and he felt sick as, and missed his mates, but it was all good.

—Wasn't it?

14

3.
At Sea: South Pacific

Survival is an art. It requires the dulling of
the mind and the senses, and a delicate
attunement to waiting, without insisting on
precision about just what it is you are waiting
for.

—Marilyn French,
The Women's Room

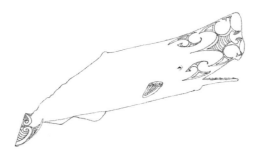

Nausea: Days 7–18

THE NEW KIWI DECKHAND AND I lie as still as possible in the cockpit during the day, baking in the unrelieved heat, hoping the inner waves of nausea will roll over us and move on, like this following sea, pushing our boat forward towards more waves and more. There is always another.

On my 9 to 12 a.m. watch I try to focus on what the Swiss French Mate is telling me in her rapid, heavily accented speech. She writes up the log and listens on the hydrophone for whale clicks so I don't have to move yet. Going below when not horizontal is death. She tells me I have a choice. I can learn to sail, or I can do what the three nannies they lost before me did and call the captain for every shift of the wind or light on the horizon.

I sit repeating to myself the names of the sails. Main. Staysail. Genoa. I have to remember what course to keep and how to get the real wind speed from the direction of the wind and the apparent speed, somehow adding up to our speed over ground. She tells me to imagine a bicycle going downhill and subtract in one direction and add in another and it makes no sense to me whatsoever. My shorts are wet from sea spray, and they've been that way for a long time. I feel too ill to do anything except the very minimum to help myself.

But the evening is cooling, and the hull is humming through the gurgle and slap of water. The Mate turns off all but the red and green running lights as she goes below. I look up at the full dome of the night sky and see the impossible stars.

Day 7

ALL IS MUCH AS USUAL in the unusual way of things. It is difficult to do the simplest things, as if feeding oneself during an earthquake might be simple. The wind has been steady and hard and the sky clear. Good sailing, to the experienced
half of the crew. The waves are anywhere from one to three meters, and often the ship is running down waves near the top of her cruising speed, around nine knots, for a few seconds before dropping back to seven or eight.

I feel as if I am pregnant: seasick every morning when I wake up and euphoric during the night when the moon is out and the waves are silver-grey and black, always shifting, unpredictable and mesmerizing. The sound of the whale comes up through the hydrophones like the carpenter fish he was once called, knocking on our hull: *toc toc toc.*

Our first sperm whale, my first and *Cachalot's* first in a month, clicked away yesterday and we turned back on our course to follow it. It is amazing in this vast desert of waves that we could find the low, off-centre blow and come within meters of the giant, wrinkled sea-creature. It dived once, we listened and followed, and again we came abreast of the animal. It wallowed for a long few moments, blew several times, showed us the very tip of its broad, notched fluke.

18

Then it—he—lifted his tail high into the air where every ragged scar and scrape was recorded by our cameras before he dived again, clicking, into the five thousand meters of sea beneath us. No females, not even plankton to green these empty miles of blue. Just the whale and us: our yacht *Cachalot*—another sort of whale—sloshing and popping about on the surface of this vast space while the sperm whale cruised easily in the still depths, graceful, searching (as we are) and calling, Where are the others?

Day 8

I AM READY FOR IT to be easier, this expedition of ours. Mornings are the worst for me; when it cools off in the afternoon, I do a little better, especially if I have time alone. A relative concept with seven people on a forty-foot boat. The heat is as constant as the wind; incredible to have both together without one mitigating the other. At night one dreams. I'm told they're normal, these enormous dreams, but is anything normal in this tiny craft of wood and fiberglass in the middle of such an emptiness of ocean that not even my dreams could have fabricated?

Every day the First Mate, Nathalie, drops a buoy that records light going down into the water and light coming back up, in effect recording any photosynthesizing plants, to measure the ocean's productivity at varying distances from where the whales feed. She drops a Secchi disk to the same effect, a white disk of plastic, weighted with lead on a line marked off in meters. It drops down into that deep blue until it disappears from view, and she counts out the meters of line while hauling it back on board. The probe is another gizmo that tells us just how very empty this ocean is. It is a gun of sorts; a hollow plastic tube that drops a bullet of lead trailing a fine copper wire, which shows up in the sun like a thin soap bubble, or an illusion, following the bullet deep into the water. It sends information to our shipboard computer, telling our Mate the temperature at given depths. Adam, the five-year-old, likes to yell out: 'Load the probe!' and giggle madly.

It's the heat that is the culprit. The thermocline, where the temperature levels out, is so deep, and the water on top so hot, that there is no turnover—no water rising from below to bring the nutrients of the deep up to the sunlight. Nutrients plus sunlight are the soup of life. Our ocean is static, profound and empty here, with only the giant whales diving deep (500 to 3000 meters) to bring up squid and fish and recycle their few nutritive components on the surface. A viciously small strand in a damaged food web. Sperm whales were once the most abundant species of whale, with the widest distribution, occurring in all oceans of the world. How many are left?

The male sperm whale, who we hoped would bring us to a group of females, spends his time as we do, traveling and searching. He echolocates underwater, and when he stops clicking, we search the horizon for his blow. We catch up to him twice, and the third time he blows so far away, we know there is no hope, and we turn *Cachalot* once again to the north, to the heat and the equator and towards Christmas

20

Island, which will bring us more of the same.

Sometimes the baby drools when I'm seasick and oh! the horror. Other times she butts her head against my chest, and I think it would all be less human without her. I wouldn't be here without her. I rarely know what she wants and never what I want. I can picture her adult already, demanding, egotistical little blonde girl with sea eyes. The boy is a sailor already, as eager to look at Peterson's *Field Guide to Coral Reefs* as he is to read *Charlie and the Chocolate Factory*. I watch his face as I read aloud and wonder if he really takes much of it in or if he just craves the sound of a voice in his service. Attention is at a premium. They are good kids in a difficult environment, as difficult as extreme poverty or indifference—although this is neither, unless it is the indifference of the ocean and the poverty of limited movement and stimulation. Too much and too little all at once. Every movement is an effort and every rhythm interrupted by apocalyptic waves suddenly throwing our world from side to side.

Day 9

IT IS A LITTLE EASIER TODAY. The wind is softer and the waves more regular. We're still heading northwest. A bird that looks very much like an immature gannet is following us. The Captain's Wife—CW— says it is a brown booby. Two now.

Whales are sacred, CW says. Meaning our time with them? The male we were following was the first they'd seen since the Marquesas. Not a good sign if they are hoping to find an increase in the whale stocks since the 1987 international whaling moratorium. It has been almost a decade. Time itself becomes sacred out here.

Ten boobies! Now seventeen! One has a white body. They seem to be generating spontaneously out of the waves off our stern, like tiny B1 bombers. They appear fascinated by us. There are at least thirty now, rising around the boat. One just sat on the water for a bare moment. Others are swirling like leaves as they turn. You can see them pull up short to keep from colliding and sometimes fighting in midair—a high-pitched *Waak-ak-ak*—dragging a single feathertip on the water like a child dragging a stick along a picket fence. One lightly pats the water with the flat of a wing, measuring the height of the uneven waves.

The baby is crying now.

Sometimes there is nothing else I am physically capable of doing besides lying horizontal in the cockpit and swapping insults with the Kiwi, Simon, while trying to entertain the kids ('carked out with the sprogs,' he'd say). Simon just called himself 'a useless lump of limp lung'. Adam is a 'stroppy ratbag', and the baby (being cuddled now by her mother down below) is a 'lovely wee chook' or 'bubbie'. Hanging out with us in the cockpit is 'better than a poke in the eye with a sharp stick', he reckons. But 'hard yakker' even so. We rock with the water and talk about home.

Day 18

LIFE FLOWS AND CHANGES, AND it is almost impossible to remember the feelings of even a moment before, unless one watches the moonstream on the waves during the early-morning watch. Three a.m. and Orion has run over the horizon while our boat sails inexorably towards Christmas Island—Kiritimati, an island in the Republic of Kiribati (pronounced *kir-ih-bahss*, our Captain says). On the charts the island is north of the equator and our Global Positioning System, GPS, counts down towards zero as the scorpion chasing Orion rises in the sky. Libra balances her scales in front of the bright chain of stars delineating the scorpion's face.

We are following a big male sperm whale. His great boxy head ploughs up out of the water and arches down to show his lumpy, bumpy back, prehistoric in every way, like the multi-spiked back of a sea serpent. How easy it is out here to put oneself in mind of the old whalers: the adrenaline rush of anticipation, the magic of sighting the blow of the beast and then the great head turning away. When he dives, we see the humped back first, wait a long moment before the tail stock begins to rise—and will the flukes lift? We wait with our cameras and our nets to scoop any little bit of skin or whale shit that might come our way, humbly awaiting the majesty of the final surge upward. The flukes curve gracefully up as they rise, lift vertically to the sun and descend with barely a ripple.

Sometimes he talks. The hydrophone is attached to a recorder, waiting for codas, the patterned signature of each individual whale. It is a busy sound, softer than the male's echolocation clicks, which clang metallically in our earphones. What must it have been like to hunt these beasts with their clicks knocking against the hulls of those aggressive little whaling boats? And how do we justify the near-eradication of these incredibly social, intelligent animals?

I DRAG ON A LINE behind *Cachalot* at about a knot and a half. Enough to pull my facemask off if I try to look behind me—looking for what? Thousands of meters of empty, sun-struck blue. A very few jellies stream past, tentacles angled every which way. I duck away from a miniature sea-lion jelly and get an itchy sting for my trouble. Most of the jellyfish are colorless and therefore, I hope, harmless. The whale is about thirty-five meters away. When I raise my head I can see him plainly, wrinkled back bobbing just above the surface. But underwater I can see only the boat, the blue, the jellyfish, and me. Earlier, the Mate had done her productivity station. Again, the water was hot on top and the thermocline deep. No turnover here, but the visibility is bad anyway.

Then I see the whale. Underwater he is a ghost, an etching of a whale, no more than a pale white line against the shifting lights of blue. He is fewer than fifteen meters away. I can see his face, not just the funny off-centre blowhole and primitive back. This bull sperm whale may have come all the way from the Arctic searching for a pod of females. He has

24

white speckling around his jaw, an intelligent eye and a remarkably canine-looking head. I think that and then don't know why. There is nothing humble or obsequious in the giant's look, just . . . familiar.

He turns towards our boat, showing me his entire profile, still the negative image, a white outline on dark blue, moving like a cartoon. The massive body lifts, the tail flukes up, and he dives in a swirl of bubbles. I snap a picture. It seems a small thing to do and unworthy of the experience.

THE DAY BEFORE YESTERDAY WE swung from a line tied from the mast to the bosun's chair hanging off *Cachalot's* port side and I saw my tiny world swing out as I floated wide like a spider on a long silk. Terrifying that one's world can be so small and suddenly just out of reach. It was a quiet, graceful moment of flight and distance until I slammed into the side of the boat and got a noseful of seawater from a following wave.

That night CW called down that there were dolphins on the hydrophone. I had just come off watch and snuggled into my bunk, but I leapt up half naked and we stumbled to the bow. The dolphins were invisible. Phosphorescent tunnels of green sparks were stuttering in our bow wave, cutting across and blanking out when a dolphin leapt high into the night air. It was special effects in slow motion, a sparkling few moments in fire and water. Then it was gone.

Sun Chasers

In their way they saw many whales sporting in
the ocean and in wantonness fuzzing up the
water through their pipes and vents, which
nature has placed on their shoulders.
                    —Sir T. Herbert's Voyages into
                        Asia & Africa, *Moby-Dick*

WE SAILED NORTH AND WEST. Halfway between
Tahiti and Kiribati we found the mothers. For three days the
South Pacific stayed flat as a frog pond, but clear and miles
deep. I can't remember now who heard them, and the
journals don't tell. At first it seemed we had a group of four,
but by dawn there were twenty-six. When the sun came fully
up, we could see sperm whale mothers and calves blowing
misty exhalations across our entire horizon. I wondered if
the big male we'd been following for a week had found the
mothers too. I hoped so. The clanging of one whale's voice
sounded lonely in all that cold and deep: a little boy banging
pots together in an empty room.

Our second calm, hot day out with the whales we
scared a juvenile, slid too close and sent a ripple of anxiety
through the water with our boat's shadow. The young sperm
whale rolled and presented her pale side, then jackknifed
down, thrashing her tail as she descended, regurgitating a
huge piece of squid at the same time. At the bow, the Mate,
Nathalie, grumbled, irritated that we'd drifted so close to the
little whale. The Kiwi, Simon, leaned dangerously out over

the rail with his net and called for help. I scrambled forward and between the three of us we managed to pull aboard the enormous hunk of squid, as thick as all my fingers spread and big enough around to cover the skylight over the Mate's forepeak cabin. The chunk created a manhole cover of tough, clear jelly, with a harder, reddish weave of fibers on top like the newly hardening shell of a lobster after molting.

It had been weeks since we'd had meat, so I wasn't joking when I offered to cook it up, an only slightly digested gift of whales. The young sperm whale had brought it up from the deep trenches below us, and from the thickness our Captain said it was possible the squid had been as long as our forty-foot sailboat. I really did want to try it. No one took me up on the offer to cook it. Later, the Mate confessed that most of the large squid were 'ammoniacal' and would have tasted 'dis-guzting'.

So after measuring and sampling and sticking our fingers into the jelly to see what it felt like, we heaved the squid back over the side, just another bit of organic matter filtering back down into the high peaks of inverted Himalayas. The captain's charts told us the trenches below us were about four nautical miles deep. Nathalie's study on whale food showed the Pacific Ocean to be empty her—arid, in a sense. A desert of ocean. These deep-diving sperm whales were possibly the only beings able to recycle matter to the surface from the great height and depth of the ocean canyons.

The sun angled westward in the sky and our twenty-six mothers and calves began to converge. Feeding groups of two, three and five, scattered at first over several nautical miles, gathered into a single pod. As they assembled, we followed. The whales formed the V of migrating geese and we sailed into the broad base of the triangle. The sun became large in the sky and the whales turned, together, and chased its light towards the west, following the broad bands of gold and yellow. The sun glared off the water with such intensity I had to hold my hand in front of my eyes and peek between my fingers to see their silhouettes against the light.

By early evening Nathalie was at the wheel and the captain was now the one at the bow with his long-lensed camera, a wild-haired Ahab urging his ship westward, yearning after the whales, hoping to catch just one more identifiable tail fluke despite the blinding light. Like chorus dancers the whales obliged, all twenty-six fluking up in formation, one after the other in an orderly cascade of motion. Our Captain shot each one when she fluked, with a camera instead of a harpoon, yet he was still intense as the long-awaited moment finally occurred. His aim, always, was to get perfect identifying shots of each perpendicular tail fluke.

He could barely keep up with the chorus line showing off their sea legs. His camera clicked away, and the Kiwi, Mate and I dipped our nets and harvested the confetti each dancer scattered, pale tissue-paper skin floating up from the whales' hides in strips and dots—the naughty dancers' dresses—left behind as they skipped away laughing. Down below, the submerged hydrophones rattled out the whales' songs while they chased the light, clicking and clanging, rattling and buzzing, a double-dozen young mothers clucking their tongues at a handsome male.

The watch shifted, and the Kiwi and I went below so he could show me how to preserve the skin samples for genetic testing back at the lab, to contribute to the *Who's Who* and the family tree. Simon scratched idly at an old peel of sunburn as he sat in a fugue state, resting from the long, hot day.

The top skin on his arm rucked up and he stared at it for a minute, then peeled away an immensely long strip of dead skin.

'This is how it's done, Yank,' he giggled, and stuck his own skin in a film container full of buffer fluid. 'Be sure you don't touch anything, or you'll contaminate the sample, right?'

The sample marked and labeled, he put it in the carrier addressed to the lab in Canada that we used for DNA analysis.

'Great White Whale,' I read over his shoulder.

'A bloody good control, I reckon,' he laughed.

'What if you find out you're related after all?'

'Well, me mum's adopted,' he said.

'You just never know.'

Alone on watch that night, I turn the directional hydrophone obsessively, following the whales with our sailboat's small motor but shutting it off every ten minutes to listen for clicks. Then all sound stops. The busy clicking—a chittering of birds—is lost in the hiss of water against the 'phones and I panic for a moment, thinking I've lost the pod.

I spin the wheel of the hydrophone, listening to every quadrant of the compass. I've been writing a letter to my mother under the spotlight of the moon, telling her not to worry, I won't be doing this forever, this wandering. I'm waiting, I tell her, to know what to do next, how to order my life. We all—except the captain—long for land, but hardly know why. I'll miss this night sky.

When it is time again, I spin the wheel, listening for clicks. There is only silence in every direction. No cheerful chatter. I picture the deep cold, dark beneath me, devoid of life. The heavy water seems to sit in my stomach. I can feel myself chilled and weighty, pressing against the wrinkled hides of the others, needing to hold warm life to myself in the presence of all that darkness.

Nothing makes me turn my head, but I look up and a huge shadow is blocking the stars. There are no clouds. An eye, set in a mountain of water-cooled flesh, is looking down on me from the dark. A mailbox the size of a pick-up truck has risen out of the water. The whale is peering over the railing of our boat, as if the ocean herself has decided to see who is riding on her back, spinning their wheels. The ocean looks at me. I look at the ocean, and her deep eye blinks. She is curious. I am breathless. The giant's eye is less than two meters away from mine. The head sinks down silently and I continue to sit and listen, wondering if I dream. In the dark anything is possible. I spin the wheel.

30

After a moment the chattering begins again. I didn't lose them: they've doubled back, come to see what's been crisscrossing over their heads on the water's thin night-skin. We are right on top of them. I spin my wheel and listen to whale talk. We sway with the waves and wait for the first light of morning.

Tea

WE ARE RATTLING AND CRASHING along in a frail caravan of wood. The desert heat has us gasping and sweating, a constant wind whipping around us with an irritable wail. Voices carve through the wind, whispering and shouting, asking the endless question: 'Whyyyy?'

'It's TIME.' A voice rises through the whistling wail. 'It's time NOW.
You can't sleep forever.'

I open my eyes to see Simon, barely outlined in the dark, bent over and earnestly trying to wake my feet with promises of cups of hot tea.

'It's just on the boil, if you'll only wake up . . .'

'Simon.' I wiggle my toes out from under the sheet and sit up.

'Agh!' He straightens suddenly. 'I never know which end is up with you!'

The air in the cabin is dense with steam from the kettle. I groan.

'I don't know what's worse, having tea or not having it.'

'Here,' he says, 'don't be a lazy git. I'll brew you a cuppa and I've already done the Listen and the Log. You're on. Dunno what yer whinging about,' he mutters, moving towards the galley. 'You're the one wanted to stand watch like the rest.'

I am wide awake now.

'I'm damned if I'll just be the nanny goat. It rots the

32

brain,' I whisper, and stick my head up through the hatch to see what the sky looks like.

Orion is lying almost on his side, the sky a velvet dome salted with stars.

'Cloud on the western horizon,' Simon warns. 'We're to stay at 280 degrees unless it's small enough to steer around. You can drop ten degrees, but you'll have to turn on the motor if you go below that with the wind where it is.'

The motor is loud and smelly and takes the serenity out of standing watch.

'Any whales?'

'Bugger all,' he says, and turns to hand me a cup of tea. He's already added milk and honey.

'You make incredibly good tea,' I say, taking a sip.

'Only bloody gumboot,' he grumbles.

I cradle my teacup and watch him for a minute while he tidies up the galley.

'You better get up there,' he frowns. I sigh and climb the ladder. I should know not to crowd someone after a mellow watch. It's the only time any of us has space to ourselves, but I almost wish the baby would wake up, so I'd have someone to cuddle. Everyone seems so stiff, untouchable.

He follows me up a minute later. I curl up in the far corner of the cockpit with my cup of tea and watch a dark patch blotting the stars on the far horizon. I hope it will go away and wonder if it's as small as it looks. It's impossible to judge distances and sizes out here on the endless night horizon. Simon throws a bucket over the side and grunts as it fills suddenly with water and drags on its tether. He hauls it up with an effort and starts to brush his teeth.

'I thought I heard something on the hydrophone earlier.'

'Oh, yes?'

'Yeh,' he snorts, 'then Nathalie came out and turned off the sodding fan.'

We'd discovered that the far-off whisper of whales could easily be confused, when heard over the hydrophone, with the static chatter of the fans in the First Mate's forward cabin.

'Oh . . .' I touch his arm as he throws the water from his bucket overboard again, sparking a glitter of phosphorescence that mirrors the brilliance overhead.

'Look, Yank,' he turns towards me abruptly. 'We've got to have a wee natter.'

'What'd I do?'

'You seem to reckon I'm this nice bloke. Well, I'm not. I've got to tell you; Adam is really getting up my nose when he leaps all over me. I'm sick of being a punching bag for a grubby five-year-old. I don't mind helping out with him, but I've got to ask you . . .' He stops, tips the bucket over the railing again. His eyes look closed in the dark. 'Why does he hate me?'

'He's smitten with you, didn't you know? That's why he's always at you.'

'He's worse when you're around.'

He sits down opposite, and we both look at the

34

growing cloud blotting out our stars.

The universe is disappearing. I tweak the rudder southish.

'What's so different between one cuppa tea and another?' Simon asks sleepily.

I can't tell him. 'You Kiwis need to explain when you mean tea the drink or tea the meal,' I say, 'because your brews are curiously good, but you cook like shite.'

He laughs.

'Simon, why are we out here?'

'I reckon,' he says slowly, 'we are here because the IWC wants to know if our whales have had enough wee whales during the moratorium for people to start noshing them again.'

I sit looking at the stars, trying to ignore the cloud eating up our patch of sky. I already knew that the IWC— the International Whaling Commission—was helping fund the research out here. I'd also noticed that the Captain and CW were both dedicated to whales in ways that sometimes seemed as much spiritually driven as biological. It seemed highly unlikely they'd want to help promote hunting again. I want to ask Simon how counting whales and recording their voices could be linked to hunting them for food, but he has come down off his night-watch buzz and is sleepily pulling himself down the ladder to his bunk.

The cloud gnaws at the stars, myths coming to life. I can so easily imagine people who spent their lives under the sky creating stories from the movement of the stars and clouds, the constant changes, the lovely bright moments and the dark threats. It is easy to forget how terrible and dynamic the sky is, when one is hidden away under roofs and the pacifying night-lights of cities. A gust of hot wind and cold rain reminds me to steer south again. The cloud nibbles the sky overhead again—and then passes by, only a small cloud in a big sky after all.

Preaching Geese & the Wallaby Martyr

MY FATHER CAME FROM AN attenuated bloodline of evangelist missionaries. After being well trained to follow in his father's wake like a hungry gull, he escaped by a wingtip when he traded God for Freud. He imagined his father might have been a conservationist, if the time had been right, because what my grandparents really wanted was to save the world. I never met my father's father, but his righteousness sometimes haunts the tone of his descendants' voices, as does my grandmother's hunger to explore, to run and find out.

I SLEPT IN ONE MORNING after watch, rocking in the bright sunlight above decks, curled in the sail bags on the forward deck. The wind shushed through the sails with such force I dreamed I was back on Mariah Island—an earlier journey alone, far from home—with the incessant wind blowing the sand in under the door and the deep blue sky through the cracks in the chimney.

During those nine months island-bound, I sometimes imagined myself one of the plainswomen going mad from the lonely beating of the wind on untempered minds. But I was merely camping in a centuries-old prison cell, a working stiff in Australia's wild parkland on the island of Mariah, with its close-cropped green grass and the wallabies dying of thirst. Their white bones lay on the ground and the grass grew over them.

Only the Cape Barren geese seemed to do all right,

drinking brackish water and sweating the salt through encrusted lime-green beaks. Sometimes we untangled fishing line from fluorescent red legs—when we could catch them—and watched the powder-grey bodies flounder away on gangrenous stumps. They did all right, considering.

One young goose, a juvenile, was with his parents much too long, his flight feathers grown in backwards over skinny wings from 200 years of inbreeding, feathers freckled with blanched white. His parents looked after him until the urge came on them to breed again and repeat the damaged genes and they chased him, fully grown but underweight, into the high bush. The other youth were already congregating, meeting and squabbling near the outflow of the tiny brackish stream, pairing for a lifetime before the upside-down summer—my winter—was out. If he ever found them, he wasn't invited to stay.

I scared him, lurking in the grass. I was brushing a monstrous centipede from my notebook, too unbelieving to worry about a sting. Not even a million legs should be long enough to cover my entire book, so just brush it away and ignore its slithy toves.

The poor scrawny goose honked and ran for new cover, only to be chased away by yet another breeding pair. No rest for the weary—or food for the damaged—and if he did breed, where would his poor twisted children go? I watched him lurking for weeks and felt guilt and sorrow and the inevitability of natural selection.

There go we all when our island-home becomes too populous to allow yet another to find its place. Will there be a ranger with no stomach for suffering to go into the bush when no one is looking and 'take care of the problem'? Out of sight, out of guilt, and I only rarely allow myself the sorrow of remembering him. His parents had a healthy nesting this year, I heard. Their genetic line was brought by convicts, 200 years ago. It is a tribute to the original three geese how well they've done, so far from the Barren Islands where the gene pool is wider. But how wide and deep does it have to be in the long run? Which runs out first? Space? Food? Or gene combinations? The goose or the egg? Death is more certain than anything I know, and I think about it as little as possible. Who can claim any certitude in anything? Once I asked for a sign and got too many.

I walked often along the beach, ten steps from the dune shack where some lucky warden had lived in sandy luxury compared with my crumbling 1.5m by 2.4m brick cell, built for fifteen-year-old convicts caught stealing bread to live. A possum came in my open door one night and helped himself to my licorice in the dark. I lit a candle at the huge, humped shape against starlight and breathed a sigh of relief when the night-wide eyes blinked blindly up at my flame. I felt welcoming then, and only made him take his plunder outside. Later, I heard him rummaging in the boxes of canned food. I finally braced the door shut after we had examined each other's motives thoroughly.

A wire food-safe kept the smaller *Antechinus* out until the morning I woke to a terrible hissing wail that kept my head under covers for a centuries-long minute. Finally, I ventured a look and found a trail of blood and urine leading from the nibbled fruit. I threw it all away and dreamed of wicked witches hawking poisoned apples—and slept again for a thousand years.

The next one to tap at my door of an evening was the Ranger, another twilight soul kept solitary and island-bound. We comforted each other with lager and night whispers, making a garden of splintered plank floors, his hands a rare feast of belonging.

In daylight I was careful to cut all the way around the tops of my food tins so the roos at the tip who caught their muzzles in these jagged traps would not be scarred by me. On the docks I lectured the little boys who were cutting their snarled fishing-line, throwing it into the water after fish that were too smart to nibble. They looked at me as if I were an impossible adult who could never understand. Looking back the same way, I felt all that fussing wrinkle my face into a mask. The handsome Ranger had the way of it, and we piled all those little men high into the ute, so they were tumbling out onto the hillsides on corners. We stretched them out in a human line over the barren windswept hill and cornered the goose family in the graveyard where a New Zealand warrior—a visiting Maori prince—had spent his days also in captivity, snared by chance in a European net that had flung its own unwanted peoples outward onto a strange world, but never set them free.

The little boys screeched and enjoyed the chase, and finally were confronted with their own handiwork when the fat goose was turned upside down, shitting mightily on the patient Ranger, who tried to wipe it off on me. They laughed until he showed them the sleek red legs turned black and green, swollen around the invisible fishing-line that cut through scaled skin to bone.

We sat on the gravestone of the prince and did what we could—too little, and far too late. The next time, I heard them fussing at the smaller boys on the docks, getting old masks on young faces that suddenly see the future. The Maori prince would have preferred to go home and raise his own children, no doubt, in the way of all things seeking immortality.

It is often remarked that tourists turn off their minds when they find themselves in a strange place as demanding of attention as a crisis, where mingle convicts and princes and ambulatory Bermuda shorts. The Ranger's wife came back to him one day—all forgiven—and I floundered back to my cell of planks and crumbling stone by the restless dunes. I watched the night eyes outside my broken doorway until the sun tipped up out of the sea.

I did all right—considering.

I TOOK MYSELF ON WALKABOUT, to see what I could of the interior. There I found a group of people in garish clothing feeding bread to a wallaby in front of an enormous sign reading:

DO NOT FEED PROCESSED FOOD
TO THE WALLABIES

I caught their attention and described one of the sights I'd seen: a little female wallaby with big liquid eyes, one swollen entirely outside its bony cage, bulging red with blood, pus weeping down her face like yellow tears. A large bump on the jawbone showed where old bread had lodged in her molars and triggered a super-fast growth like a spongy catacomb, trapping infection and sealing her fate at the hand of the kind Ranger, who couldn't stand suffering before death—unless it spared him a little loneliness.

The colorful travelers stared at me with their pale, flat eyes and continued feeding the wallaby bread and cooing at its woolly cuteness. You can't tell anyone anything, really, outside of their experience—but what's to do: shut them out and not try? I could become an irritating, preaching evangelist more easily than not. I can feel it growing in my jaw like the abscess on that wally, finally popping my eyes out in shock at my own hypocrisy.

Oh, but you should have seen those others, those earlier tourists, when the furious Ranger came out and shot the sick wally before their very eyes, gore on the green grass. She died a martyr. That righteous Ranger was not one to hold back, angry at a useless death. He made those pissed-off tourists scream 'animal rights' before rubbing their noses in their handiwork until they were sick with remorse, then angry at the unknown hand, the general evil, quickly forgetting their own transgressions. They pardoned themselves for their ignorance and it was a vast and encompassing . . . what was that word again?

Ah, yes: forgiveness.

42

AND WHEN I WOKE ABORDSHIP I realized I was migrating back towards that southern land, and the destination had been in my mind all along.

Perhaps.

WE HAVE BEEN AT SEA for weeks and not one day has gone by free of doubts and questions. Why are we here? Where are we going? Nights are a little better. But when, suddenly, the entire Pacific Ocean turns into a sea of glass, it is so flat and calm one can follow the light into the deep beginnings of the three-mile trenches, see odd constellations of combjellies floating like dust motes in a sunbeam.

The Mate's Tale

OKAY, YOU CAN MAKE FUN of my accent, and I say what accent? And you can say that I am short, and I don't know what you mean. But you want to hear this and no one else will tell you, so you should show great respect and listen to me while you have the chance. And while you are at it, pass the toddy *if* you please, and a splash more rum as well, thank you very much. A little more. No point in wasting good coconut. Neither good rum.

So, who came on the trip when we start out? I am aboard always, of course, and the captain, his wife with her brand-new doctorate, and their two kids. In the beginning, in Florida, there was an old friend of the captain, who was crew, and one German Nanny.

What we did was start preparing the boat for maybe ten days, maybe a week. We get ready, stock up, and then we leave. Just two days out of Florida, the engine goes *phutt*, so we turn around and come back again. This takes maybe two or three days more. After this tremendous, long time at sea, the Nanny decide that was it, she just had it, she couldn't cope any more. She decides this was absolutely enough, and she took the plane and left.

The old friend lasts a bit longer; we still keep on doing things for the boat. The captain tries to repair the engine; we are all cleaning the boat and doing stuff like that. Then, after a few days, the friend just says 'no' and he go too. He had already done several sailing trips with the captain, so he think he know what he is getting into. But then suddenly

44

it is too stupid—he is taking a year off, he is not getting paid, and he is not enjoying it. So he decides, what the hell, I go.

This trip is different. They are so tight and so nervous because of the long year ahead, that the ambience at the beginning was much worse than any other trip they did before. Everyone was just very anxious. None of the other trips were this long. In 1987, I think it was, they did a very long trip, maybe six months, in the Galápagos. That was when the boy was born, during the earthquake. But I don't think the Captain friend stayed the entire six months, so he hadn't such a long experience.

So then they must look for new people, but we were in a rush, we had to go quite soon. So what we got was another friend, who came down just for help in general. She was supposed to be nothing special, just a hand on the boat, neither crew nor Nanny, because there was not supposed to be any whale work in Panama. So she was there just for the few weeks' sail between Florida and Panama. I think these two weeks were the worst of the whole trip. Just very, very hot and slow. Not at all nice.

In Panama that friend left too, but that was planned: she was supposed to be there only these two weeks. While we were still in Florida, they manage to find a new crew member and a new Nanny who couldn't come to Florida on two days' notice, but they joined in Panama. The new Nanny was Swiss–German, but I have no recollection of her name. Maybe I think of it in a minute. The guy was named John. So we left Panama, and arrived at Galápagos, and already both of them were very, very unhappy. The Swiss–German woman, ooh, she hated sailing, and this John didn't look as bad as her, but then he left the boat without saying a word in Galápagos. That was in Puerto Ayora, the main port more or less. Puerto Ayora is where the Darwin Station is.

The day before we leave, we were supposed to do the shopping, and the captain was supposed to do all the paperwork for Customs. So we were all getting absolutely ready to leave. The night before that, John says he is going to sleep on the beach, and the captain say, 'Don't forget to put your passport on the chart table because I need to do all the paperwork tomorrow,' and John say, 'No problem, I will do that.' So he didn't sleep on the boat and in the morning the captain look on the chart table to do the paperwork and he couldn't find John's passport, so the Captain was kind of unhappy. The rest of us went to do the shopping and we were supposed to meet John at eleven o'clock in the supermarket, so we wait for him and wait for him and wait for him, and he never arrive!

And then the captain came to find us and, because we didn't know that the passport wasn't there, we say to him, 'We don't understand where this guy is, we are waiting for him,' and the captain say, 'This stupid guy didn't leave the passport!'

Then it just jumped to me, and I say, 'Did he take anything else?' and the captain say, 'I dunno, I didn't check.' And I say, 'Okay, let's go to the boat and see what's left.' We go, and there is nothing of his stuff left—no oilskin, no nothing. I say, 'Well, he is gone.' But the Captain say, 'No! Why?' And I say, 'I dunno, but none of his stuff is here.'

'Oh, but maybe he needed his oilskin and all that on the beach . . .'

And I say, 'Oh, get reality.'

So, yes! It seems that John is completely gone. That's pretty good story, ah? We couldn't leave the boat anymore. No point in doing the shopping. We didn't have a crew member. We had only four days in port, and I imagine that it took John all of these days to decide what he was doing. But I didn't have a clue, because he looks a bit like the Nanny maybe—not very happy—but he didn't look it as strong, in fact, and, for example, the day he was going to sleep on the beach, he still went out to eat with us.

So the Nanny was stuck on board because she couldn't just leave after that, she didn't feel it was right, but she was still very unhappy. The captain starts looking everywhere for somebody else, and he found a guide, a naturalist, from the Galápagos. Not a woman, at all, who knew about sailing in difficult water. She had no clue about sailing. She had a clue about being at sea but for very short days only because she is just a naturalist. You know, they just go out with the tourists and go around the islands and show them the seals, show them the sea lions, show them this and that. Just like you, in fact. And now you get to be the Nanny. Ha!

This naturalist was Ecuadorian, and she was quite keen to come along. The captain is very well known in the Galápagos, which always sounds quite good, and she thought it was a great opportunity. So she come to us with absolutely no long sailing experience, no nothing, just interested in whales or interested in biology in general. And, ah! She hated it after a few days. So the three of us, the Nanny, and Peppi—that was her name—were always just chatting and chatting in Spanish or in French because the boat was not yet speaking all the same language. And because of this, I knew that things were not completely happy with the boat.

When we arrived at the Marquesas, Peppi and the Swiss German, they wanted to leave. But the Captain convince them to stay aboard until we arrive to Tahiti.

From Galápagos to Marquesas, it is, 2500 to 3000 nautical miles? It is a long way. The longest stretch. We took about three weeks, I think, but sailing very, very quickly. In terms of nautical miles, it's absolutely huge. We didn't see a single whale: no nothing. So in fact Peppi, who wanted to see whales, didn't get very much out of that neither.

To me, the weather was perfect. We had the trade winds. We were just zooming at ten knots, maybe eight knots on the boat speedometer plus two knots of current, just zooming down to the Marquesas, with that absolutely beautiful trade wind always blowing from behind. So the weather was very, very good. And the whale sightings were nonexistent.

We saw whales just after Panama, which was the only time we saw them, then we heard them once around the Galápagos and we heard one—only a single click— somewhere in the middle between Galápagos and Marquesas, but we didn't see it at all. So the only sighting before Tahiti was the one near Panama. That's bad, ah?

We did sight, very quickly, one whale between the Marquesas and Tahiti. I don't think we managed to take any picture of it, but that one whale gets me in big trouble. Here we are with absolutely no meat aboard, eating nothing but disgusting lentil every meal. No wine to drink. And the Captain and his Wife are saying, 'We have a whale!' and I say, 'Very good, that is what we look for,' and I call to this whale I cannot see, 'Swim close, little whale, and I will carve a steak!' Well, you can imagine! I think perhaps they never speak to me again. Maybe not so bad, eh?

Both Peppi and the Nanny stay on, both unhappy, and in Tahiti, the minute we arrive, they just put their bags on the shore.

And then the new Kiwi crew and Yank Nanny arrive in Tahiti.

AND NOW YOU SAY, NATHALIE adds, from our sandy beach-bed on a not-quite-deserted island where we were marooned not a month after setting sail from Tahiti—now you say they tell you from the start they don't want a sailor, don't want someone interested in whales, ask you to look after their two kids in the worst condition in the world, on this teeny, dirty boat. For barely any pay. Eating nothing but lentil. And you say *yes*? No wonder the captain doesn't want to anchor near any island that have an airport.

4.
Republic of Kiribati: October

The rule of the road
is a paradox quite
though custom has proved it so long.
If you go to the left, you go right
If you go to the right, you go wrong.
—Henry Erskine

Two Journals In the Doldrums: Days 27-49

Day 27

WE ARE SAILING AWAY FROM Kiritimati. I'm sorry to see it fade into that collapsing line between sea and sky. Four days stranded by high winds on a tropical island and now back on the whale road again. My journal stayed aboardships with most of our crew, so I will write up our first landfall as I remember, and time allows. The sea is flat, the wind sparse, and the crew who were left aboard are grumpy.

When we first arrived, *Cachalot* followed a pod of dolphins in towards the coast and spent the night anchored off the windy side of the island. In the morning all of us but the captain rowed ashore the long way, around a point into a protected harbor.

Kiritimati seemed poor and dirty at first glance. The English used the island for upper-stratosphere H-bomb testing; the Americans came after and abused it in the same way, to the detriment of millions of seabirds. Now it is being used by the people of the Gilbert and Solomon Islands because they have excess population and little land. Later on, one of the local expats told us the army types were the ones who trashed the place.

Underneath the piles of rusting machinery is a coral island heavily wooded in coconut trees and surrounded by rich reefs with their own hidden dangers. One day we saw giant tooth marks on a big man's skin, tattoos stitching his entire torso and back. He ran at us yelling when he saw Nathalie and me wading along the perimeter of the bay. We couldn't understand what he was saying until he pointed to the scars. 'Don't wade in the shallows' was written all up and down his back. I decided that I wouldn't be diving to set *Cachalot's* anchor again in a hurry.

I'm so tired I doubt I'll catch up my journal tonight, but I'm looking at a goddess's foot hanging astern, a pandanus, looking like a huge clump of candy corn, each toe —each kernel—the size of my fist. That particular goddess must have had some nasty bunions. I can picture one of the local children twisting the giant pandanus fruit from her neighbour's tree, stealing it for us in the dark last night, knowing we would set sail today.

Day 28

SIMON SAYS:
Here we are, sailing on Cachalot's *Cut-rate South Pacific Tour once again. Three weeks at sea to see four days of land —from a safe distance. The wenches are back on board, covered in flowers, and we are all shuffling off to Samoa. While they lounged on shore, the rest of us spent days popping about in the surge with constant, unending, fussy kid care. We did fill half our tanks with water from the only other visiting yacht's reverse-osmosis water filter.*

We have fish and coconut from the women's enforced stay ashore, but little else except a large and dangerous fruit hanging astern where a friendlier hand of bananas traveled from Tahiti. The bloody plant throws large seeds out randomly at a rate of knots. It pongs like rotten puha. It will soon get turfed overboard if I have anything to say about it.

Day 29

OUR SHIP'S LOG READS:

Sperm Whale Encounter No. 13

Reason for leaving: A Single Male eluded us [as is often the case in my experience].

Area: Line Grounds West, nr Jarvis Island [Kiritimati is a dream in the distance].

Encountered: Acoustically [you heard it here, folks].

Sea Temp: 27.7 Celsius [plenty warm, if only some people would stop for a swim].

Depth: 5000 meters [plenty deep, don't look down].

Notes: Single Male heard during encounter with spotted dolphins, doing usual clicks while diving, a few slow clicks. Moving north. A couple distant lobtails, seemed spooked by our engine—did a series of shallow dives when we approached within 600 m—then silent. Looked large at a distance [and then he was gone].

OUR FIRST DAY ON KIRITIMATI, Nathalie and I stayed ashore and got stranded by the weather. The Gilbertese we met took us in, fed us, gave us coconut tea and toddy. The coconut is an amazing plant: most of the drinking water seems to be filtered through it, and they make a syrup from the sap that is similar in consistency to maple syrup. I'm eating the thin, almost flabby flesh from one of the young coconuts we stacked on deck. One of the local women thought it was hilarious when I offered to pay her kids to bring us a couple of bags for the boat. 'No one pays for coconut!' she said.

When we first moored off the island, it was a tough row in *Cachalot's* little dinghy just to get to shore. I held the baby in the bow while Simon and CW rowed, mostly staying put as the current drew us backward. I watched a tree on land stay in the same place for so long, I didn't think we'd ever reach shore. The outer surf was bad—we were trying to go around it into the mouth of a harbor guarded by a rip. When we finally landed, I leapt out to secure the boat and landed smack on my butt in three feet of water. Nathalie took off immediately while Simon and I waited with itchy feet for CW and the kids. Walking freely on a solid surface felt like finding religion. My feet seemed to have a deep and abiding belief that solid ground felt *right*.

We'd landed our dinghy on a sandy beach with scattered coconut palms. A man was fixing a pigpen holding a cluster of runty red and black piglets, half-baked by the sun. A little boy about Adam's age watched with big eyes from a palm-frond hammock and a few teens came out and stared, but no one said anything. It was intimidating, coming in by the back door of the island. There was a smudge fire drying coconut halves, with others set out in neat, dotted lines. A group of people were standing around the fire. As soon as we started walking towards them, a woman darted up and grabbed our baby girl and ran off with her to the group drying copra. CW stood watching, arms at her sides. A tense moment later the woman came running back, carrying the baby gingerly by the armpits while she wailed. When she stopped crying, someone else scooped her up again, laughing.

I walked towards a smiling woman who, as I advanced, seemed to shrink back. She had the most beautiful brown and gold child in her arms. I asked about phones and showers and stores, none of which seemed even the vaguest possibility in that landscape of sand and tin-roofed shacks and drying copra.

Maharua, the woman with the beautiful child, spoke perfect, quiet English. Everyone worked for the government here in London Town, she told us: no phone until Monday, no stores, no shower unless we would follow her to her house? Simon, CW and I followed; courtesy demanded it. The house was open at two ends with closed rooms lining each side, each with a weathered blue door. We walked on through to a dirt yard and there was a shallow stone well— just a few rocks holding back the sand—with scoops made from cut milk jugs. 'No rain,' Maharua said. We didn't want to take her drinking water (as we thought, not knowing about the filtering properties of the coconut tree) but we didn't want to be rude. 'We'll return later?' we asked, and she waved. 'Anytime,' she said. We walked. It felt wonderful.

Maharua put us on a deep sand road that soon turned into pavement lined with the ever-present coconut. Then we turned a corner into the town and saw the trash. Not Gilbertese trash—English trash, American trash, the detritus of years as a nuclear test site. Those rusted hulks of metal and enduring plastic struck us, then, as signs of great poverty. The Gilbertese ignored them. They had coconut and fish and land. No one was hungry. They had contact with other islands by boat and a plane came in once a fortnight with mail and canned goods. They had two churches to battle for their souls.

Two men drove by in a dusty pick-up and stopped to stare when they saw us trudging up the road. We needed information. I walked up and asked what they could tell us about the island. They gave us a ride to their 'hotel', an ex-army barracks far out of town near the single landing-strip. We had long, luxurious, cold showers, fed the baby, saw very little of the local life, and finally caught a ride back towards town and the dinghy. We caught up with Nathalie at the turn-off to Maharua's house.

'I am not going back,' she said, very clipped and Swiss/French. 'You would like to stay with me?'

'Where?' I asked.

'A Frenchman and an Englishman have invited me to dinner. I will sleep at the Catholic mission.'

'I'm tempted,' I said, looking at CW, who looked crestfallen.

'Sure,' CW said, and she and Simon and the kids went back to the dinghy.

That was the last we saw of them for the next four days. An eternity. A joy.

Day 30

SIMON SAYS: *So Today is Tomorrow, when I should be writing about Yesterday, a completely run-of-the-mill, mundane and routine day in which nothing at all of interest occurred. As I am actually writing this several days later, I hesitate to suggest that I recall a blind thing anyway. I did try to work on the stats for my thesis, but with little success. Made a rattling good start but couldn't get enough time or space alone to concentrate. I feel as thick as two short planks, actually. Sometimes I feel guilty about picking out on the albatross/shearwater project and leaving my mates back home with all the work. Getting anything done out here on a rolling boat, with wee sprogs wriggling about like maggots on a hotplate, the head door slamming, riot and mayhem . . . Hard cheese. May try again later, but somehow, I doubt it. Just can't be bothered.*

Day 31

IT'S BEEN HARD TO READJUST to the boat after our brief time on Kiritimati. The crew left aboard were angry with us; I'm still not quite sure why. CW said she understood we couldn't help the wind coming up but said that I'd been too excited about being on land. She reminded me rather angrily that my stated objective was sailing. I tried to tell her my imagined definition of sailing included *landing* in new places occasionally. We both raised our voices. We get so little *time*; I feel it should at least be guilt-free. I eventually said I was just hungry for new experiences, not to mention seasick.

CW finally admitted she hadn't gotten what she needed this landfall and maybe would take more time on the next. She implied that I'd had my time; next landfall would be her turn. Now I am left dreading that they will expect me to be on kid-watch constantly and I will never have another break.

Nathalie claims that the captain doesn't like land. The family doesn't seem as organized on land as at sea, and the time just dribbles away with small concerns. She says the captain will promise four days on land, with two off, but if all the work gets done in two, then he changes his mind and the boat sails on. She recommends that I take my free time first —then do my time with the kids while the crew restocks the boat. Unsurprisingly, I'm still waffling about whether to continue with the expedition after New Zealand.

Some of the help I got early on with the kids has dried up, although Simon still lends a hand. He spends the rest of his time sleeping or reading and is often bored, I think. He is hooked into the science, though, seems tracked into the academic system in New Zealand, but says he wants to stay on board until the boat returns to Canada. Doesn't know if he can afford to, but he was invited to do the whole trip while Nathalie and I were slacking off on the island (marooned is another word). I have often felt that no matter how hard I work, it is never enough. My father always warned us that what everyone in the world is really looking for is a servant to look after them—or a wife.

Adam is having a major temper tantrum down below. At least the stinky dried fish cooked up into a tasty soup for supper. Life ain't all bad. The good things out here are the phosphorescence trailing from our rudder like a miniature Milky Way, its stars flashing nova. Dancing on watch. Singing harmony with CW over the dishes, insulting Simon, and cooking with Nathalie. Getting hugged by the baby and young Adam's smile when he looks you in the eye. The captain's rare humor. Not feeling seasick every now and then. The 12 to 3 a.m. watch when I've had some sleep, I am alert enough to think, and no one else is awake.

WE SAW DOLPHINS YESTERDAY. Two different groups of spotted *Stenella*. The first group was made up of bigger animals; most of them had yellow, medallion-sized blisters on their sides. The second group was smaller, darker individuals with raw red gashes and odd circles and lumps marring their hides. Pollution? Cookie-cutter sharks? CW says she doesn't think there is much pollution out here, but I've read that the top few millimeters of all the oceans are polluted now, like the skin on a glass of warm milk. It is a small, enclosed ecosystem.

SAME DAY, LATE AFTERNOON. AN hour's grace. Damn seasickness pill made me sleep away most of my free time. People seem unmotivated lately, and it is hot. We're heading north again, zigzagging to find the whale. Simon says we are a quarter of the way to Samoa, but Nathalie says we'll use up our forward progress by heading north. I was so sure I heard a big pod of whales last night until the captain switched off the fans in Nat's cabin. Static electricity was calling from the deep.

When I get down about this sailing expedition, Nathalie tells me about others she's been on where it sounds like they spent most of their time eating. Apéritifs: gin and tonics at sunset. That's not quite what I'm looking for either. I liked who I was on Kiritimati, talking to people with such confidence, taking what they offered when we were stranded, exchanging stories. Why can't I do that everywhere? Does deprivation really build character and drive? I'd hate to believe that.

Day 32

SIMON SAYS: *Had a go at cooking sweet and sour cabbage for tea, but as half the ingredients were missing, it ended up somewhat strange. Honey, lemon juice and cumin worked surprisingly well together, really. Made a massive pot of rice with sultanas for pudding, which was spot on. There was enough left over so that we can nosh at it all day tomorrow as well. Bloody oh yeah, mustn't forget the awesome reconstituted spuds that accompanied the mess. Nothing like powdered potatoes in seawater. Finally turfed the pandanus fruit overboard today. No one except Adam ate the seeds as far as I could tell and all he did was suck them and leave them lying about the place. Like most of the food aboard, you can live on it . . . but.*

Day 33

GIVING A WHOLE NEW LIFE to the phrase 'ships passing in the night' in this desert of an ocean, a brightly lit fishing boat passed us. A big one, according to Simon, and less than a kilometer away. Nathalie hasn't been feeling well, so saintly Simon took double watch without waking her. I was dreaming I was in some cowboys-and-Indians-type television show—the kind of dream you think is real until the subtitles come up. I even thought I was awake until Simon shook me to do my watch.

It was rocky earlier in the night. Lots of spray through the hatch, spitting onto yours truly while I was trying to fall asleep. Later the wind came up too, and everything was flapping and groaning and gurgling and creaking. Only half awake, I was convinced that *Cachalot* was living up to her name and we'd all been swallowed whole and were being digested in a giant whale's stomach. I was relieved when the engine went on and masked the rest of the noises. How could I ever have thought sailboats were quiet?

Simon made another good cuppa tea. The ship that passed in the night was still large on the horizon when I finally got up to take watch.

A little heat lightning is playing the sky to port now as I write. The stars are mirrored again in the phosphorescence in our wake, their miniature living solar systems flashing into existence and dying in the expansion and contraction of watery galaxies.

We're swinging around a lot now, but at least the

wind has died down a bit. Impossible that we've only been gone from Kiritimati for six days. Our pandanus fruit, hanging over the cockpit, started ripening to the point where the 'toes' were exploding off the stem. Bit of a hazard. They hurt when they hit. Simon chucked it all overboard this morning—or was it yesterday? I wish he hadn't. I liked the idea of sucking on a god's toes for my vitamin C. I did swim then, during Nathalie's station, the sea empty except for hundreds of almost invisible combjellies shaped like little lightbulbs with two tails. I'm scared of the sea wasps I've read about but wouldn't know if I'd seen any. I'm pretty chicken all round. I hung on to the ladder, staring down into 4000 meters of empty, sun-struck blue water, not even trying to swim free of the boat until I saw the captain do it. It's like leaving the one solid point in space. Mama.

When I floated free of her, *Cachalot* looked so small against that unrelieved horizon. I couldn't make myself swim more than ten, twenty strokes off the stern and then I headed back at top speed when I felt her pulling away. Exercise is like vegetables now—at a real premium. Lord, how I crave salad! Nathalie got all clever and used some of the hated beans to grow sprouts. She put oil and tons of pepper on a bowlful and handed it to me. I've never tasted anything so good.

NO WHALES: WEATHER'S TOO ROUGH even if we found them. Wish I had more time to read about them. My sailing skills aren't exactly expanding in leaps and bounds either. Nathalie is teaching me the constellations and someday how to use the sextant. Mostly, I'm the Nanny. It still bothers me when the captain talks about four rather than five scientists on board. As if he feels he has to reiterate that point to protect CW's interests. Still, I guess I've made my choices.

There is a faint but decided glow just east of north. An island? Another ship? Also a flashing point of light above it, an airplane heading east. Busy out here tonight. The sky is more entertaining than I ever imagined. How will I ever live under a roof again?

Day 34

SIMON SAYS: *Time drags like a rat's arse.*

Day 35

IT HAS BEEN A WEEK since Christmas (Island). We are solidly back in boat mode, except there are no whales. Nathalie has had a headache for four days now and I'm getting one myself. All the same, we follow a schedule, and it seems to work, keeps us moving forward through the waves. Last night, as the moon came up, there were dolphins zigzagging through the phosphorescence. They are more visible in the dark than they are in daylight. We could see even the dim tracks of the deep swimmers and an occasional blast of green went up like fireworks from the bow riders, streams of sparks marking their trails as they dived and leapt. I slept with strange dreams until dawn, and there were the positives of our negative night dolphins still swimming off the bow. Tursiops maybe, large and dark with a greyish wash along their sides, and the sky a morning pastel foil.

I'M BEGINNING TO FORGET WHAT it felt like to be on land. Back on Kiritimati—Christmas Island, so named when Captain Cook landed on the then uninhabited island on Christmas Eve 1777—Nathalie and I shared a big double bed surrounded by mosquito netting in the empty Catholic mission. The Father was away visiting his home country, we'd been told. The sheets were fragile and ripped and the windows slatted shut. I shut Nathalie out once when I went to bed early and she finally gave up knocking and went around to the window and called in her it's-time-for-watch voice, 'Yan-Qui!' My sleepy mind had refused to answer until I heard that note. Another time we got to giggling and talking well into the morning. Once it got too light to go out and pee in the yard, it was torture until Fred-the- Frenchman next door woke up and unlocked the toilet. But the first night was the real magic: dinner with the expatriates.

Perry was an Englishman once, he said. He was in his early sixties and married to a Gilbertese woman named Erena. She looked not a day over thirty-five but was in fact fifty, so he said. When we walked into her yard the first night, Erena got up from her woven mat on the cement pad in front of her wall-less house and welcomed us to her outdoor table. I handed her a loaf of bread I had bought in town, and she asked if I wanted it prepared for us. I said no, the bread was for her, and she hugged me as if I'd done something

66

unexpected. Fred, Nathalie, Perry and I sat at the table and tried every kind of coconut drink known to the island. Erena and her daughters cooked outside, next to the table, in a split fifty-gallon drum. Late in the evening, when the food was ready, she waved us over to help ourselves. She would not eat with us, although I pressed her to. She finally sat with us but refused absolutely to drink at the same table as her husband.

A young man who had been schooled in mechanics in the Solomons and in California (or perhaps that was a hope for the future) came over to talk and brought with him our first fermented toddy, *karewe*, made from the sap of the coconut tree. Most of the trees had Coke bottles strung up high in the leaves, collecting sap. Fred warned us not to try to climb any of the trees that did not have these bottles, as the steps cut into the trunk would not be as fresh and old steps tended to get slippery with mould. (I did in fact try both sorts the next day, much to the amusement of Erena's flock of children.) When Erena took me to the outhouse late in the evening, I found it was one of the very few locked buildings on the island (Fred's place being another). Toilet paper was expensive and doled out in careful squares.

Perry was the one who talked the most that evening. He had been working for the government but was now retired and relied on Erena's dry goods 'store' to get by. The store was a shuttered window in the side of their house with a very small stock of canned goods—two cans of peas, four of peaches and half a dozen cans of Spam—that looked rather lonely on otherwise empty shelves. Erena said a few words about buying a boat to do trading through the islands in future, but Perry quickly said no, they were on Christmas to stay.

The two of them had done yacht delivery and trading before, usually combining both while carrying bicycles from island to island. His job with the government had been to help set up a relocation programme for the overcrowded islands of the Gilbertese group. Christmas was seen as a very good spot, even compared with Fanning Island, he said. Christmas had the buildings left by the various army testing people out by the little airstrip near a town named Banana. Government jobs were available in London Town, Poland and Paris, across the bay. They had an incredibly rich supply of fish offshore, plenty of coconuts, and, if one wanted, land of one's own on the more remote peninsulas. Land brought all of them here. Their only complaint, these people from the Gilbert group, was that their days were too hot and the nights too cold.

The laid-back atmosphere of our arrival disappeared on Monday when all the offices opened, and sure enough, London Town wasn't a tin-shack ghetto after all but a working government station. It was a significant change after a night of watching hordes of children dancing to rap music from a dusty tape-deck in Erena and Perry's cement yard. The kids had gathered around the boom-box just outside our circle of adults that first night. One at a time, each child got up and danced while the others clapped. By the time we got up from dinner to go with Fred to the mission, most of the kids were asleep where they lay, on woven palm-frond mats or just curled up naked on the cement platform under the sky.

In contrast, Fred-the-Frenchman's place was pretty posh: four wooden walls and a room full of bunk beds and indoor plumbing. He said the Catholic Father had had the cabin built just for him, but there was a hostel sign hanging outside over the door. Just for men, he said then, and really just for him. Fred gave us our lodgings at the mission, but the next day he told us he wanted us out and made sure he repeated himself often until the wind let up and we finally left. But I'm getting ahead of myself again. Or behind. Ah, I thought I was over this stupid seasickness.

Day 36

SIMON SAYS: *One quarter of the way to Pago Pago, American Samoa, we change our course from SW to NW to enter the eastern fringes of big whaling grounds. This means we are heading away from our next island destination and making it, in fact, harder to get there. Some surprised looks all round, though this itinerary was planned from the beginning. One automatically expects to be heading towards land, but for the captain, whales are his destination. So on we go on our gentle, lethargic wee cruise. Set the sails for a week and read. Adam needs a good kick up the bum and some stronger discipline. There is just no reasoning with a five-year-old.*

Day 37

SHIP'S LOG SAYS:

    Sperm Whale Encounter No. 14

    Reason for leaving: Male lost, hard to follow as made few clicks.

    Area: On the Line, Grounds West, north of Phoenix Islands.

    Encountered: Acoustically.

No Data Collected.

    Sea Temp: 28.2 Celsius **Notes:** Several short, slow clicks heard—hard to directionalize.

[Whales, unlike children, should be heard if not seen.]

WE ARE SITTING ON A most uncooperative whale that's not clicking often enough for us even to get a bearing. Nathalie stayed up for my whole 9 to 12 watch last night. She told great recipes as if they were epic poems, and I told Greek myths while she showed me her own constellations. I tried to come up with myths to fit her stars.

    Yesterday was really good. No seasickness. The kids were mellow, and we had a real swim. The boat hove to and Simon, Nathalie, Adam and I jumped overboard into the deep blue. I was the only one with a mask. The others said it was too scary to actually see what wasn't below them. Diving down and spiraling up through the sunbeams was heavenly and quiet. Found some more small, weirdly shaped jellies but saw no other life at all. Afterwards, Simon, Nat and I had two whole beers each and sat in the afternoon sun eating anchovy olives from one of Nat's preciously hoarded tins. Ever so civilized. I had some time to myself earlier on the prow listening to my music and reading. 'The Love Song of J. Alfred Prufrock' comes through for me on every journey.

'I should have been a pair of ragged claws, scuttling across the floors of silent seas . . .'

I HAVE MIXED FEELINGS ABOUT finding whales at this point. But today I was tired after an early-morning watch and the kids were aggressive and I just didn't want to be in Nanny mode all day. Thankfully, the Captain took kid-watch on time, despite imminent cetaceans on the horizon, and I got another hour's sleep. When I read about the whales, I feel more hooked into *Cachalot's* research goals, and it is easier to continue.

This leg of the trip makes our expedition feel almost over, as halfway points tend to do, yet Nathalie tells me we've zigged so far west in our northern zag that we may have to really fight to get back down to Samoa because of the trade winds. Especially if the wind stays SE, which it is now. Our food seems very low. The bean farts begin.

Nathalie's thirtieth birthday is in a fortnight or so. 'I grow old . . . I grow old . . . I shall wear the bottoms of my trousers rolled . . . Do I dare to eat a peach . . .'?

Believe me, if we had any peaches in this blasted galley, I would dare.

Day 38

SIMON SAYS: *FOUND A LONE MALE yesterday. The Captain's arse for a cabbage if I could photograph it properly or find any whale skin. Just not happening. My night watch was disastrous too. I spent the whole time dashing around in circles trying to follow the whale. I got bloody stressed and made a cockup of it all. But I did keep up somehow. I sussed out this morning that some other whales came near us, and as a result I got all bollixed up following one, then another, all the while thinking they were the same whale. Nearly sent me round the twist. Following a single whale is a piece of piss usually, even though when it comes to the surface and stops clicking, you've got up to twenty or thirty minutes when you don't know where it is. A truly stressful ruddy time. It is scorchingly hot now the sun is up. Even the water temp is an unbelievable thirty degrees Celsius.*

Day 39

MOBY-DICK AIN'T SO BAD. I think every single person aboard—except the kids—brought a copy, but no one seems to manage to plough right through to the end. But one can dip into it as into poetry and always find a timely moment.

> 'Oh, the rare old Whale, mid storm and gale
> In his ocean home will be
> A giant in might, where might is right,
> And King of the boundless sea.'

Day 40

SIMON SAYS: SHIT-HOT DAY CRUISING with the whales. Following a group of fifteen to twenty whales with six to eight in any one cluster at a time. We followed that slow-clicking male to find this group but haven't got a squiz at any males around since. Jocd-out for a three-hour sleep in the middle of the day because had been up since 0300. We collected a heap of skin samples (around forty) and several choice fluke shots. All up, a good day, especially as I missed the hottest part of the bloody thing. Everyone got a wee bit tense towards the end. Combination of poor sleep and heaps of sun, I reckon. We are still 800-plus nautical miles from Pago Pago. At least these whales are swimming SE like the clappers, which is exactly where we want to go. Crikey, I'd love to catch up with everyone at home again. Research is finally going full tilt just as our food is getting limited.

Day 41

A TYPICAL DAY WITH WHALES: I am on constant kid-watch and relieved of night watch for this period. I miss it. I wake up just before 6 a.m. (voluntarily, more or less) and fold away my sheet and turn my bunk into a day seat. I listen to Adam slam the head door loudly in Simon's ear (he's trying to sleep just across the cabin) and try to get to the head myself before the baby wakes up (usually don't make it). I pull her out of the net before she manages to pry her mom's eyelids off, and balance her on my hip while I mix her bottle and stuff something (anything) in my mouth to ward off seasickness. Then, carefully, balance the baby up the ladder to the cockpit and strap her into the legless highchair. Did I remember her harness?

Day 42

SIMON SAYS: *WE LEFT THE WHALES. Weather deteriorated and it was ruddy hard to follow them. We're now sailing flat tack to Pago Pago, bearing 150 degrees, ETA five to seven days dependent on weather, distance about 720 nautical miles. Got a squiz at three whales head-to-head, one upside down and showing a pink lower jaw. Quite startling. They didn't seem to be doing much except slapping their tails sideways during the time we were following. (Whales playing slap and tickle?) Note: Creaks may be followed by side fluking; they seem somehow related. Could side fluking be related to mating? (Reckon it must be, in some instances.) Perhaps the female was rolling onto her back to prevent mating? It's all guesswork.*

Looking forward to our break in US Samoa. Hopefully, it will be long enough to get chocolate and decent food. Everyone is happy to be rattling south again. Heard some more whales but ignored them. Just sailed on past. Couldn't quite believe it. I was well away with the fairies when I realized I had a stunning headache, so spent the arvo carked out.

I didn't wake up for two days.

Day 43

RE LAST ENTRY: TYPICALLY OF a typical day—got interrupted. And again . . .

Quotes for the Day:

CW: 'You're putting me on the spo-ot.' 'A quote? Okay. Life is, umh—there.'

NATHALIE: 'Di doop.' 'Yidoo.' 'Etwas ZO gut [good].' 'Not et all.' 'In fact.' 'Is *terri*ble.' '*Dis*-guzting.' 'Can you imagine?'

ADAM: 'For heaven's *sakes*, Nathalie!' 'Oh my heavens!' 'Quick as a wink.' 'Busy, busy as a bee, I won't be home for supper.'

SIMON: 'Adam, you little grub.' 'Going to *Sam*-oa.' 'It's pronounced wal-*russes*, ya dag.' 'That would be choice.'

THE CAPTAIN: 'Okay, I can do the log for you.'

THE BABY: 'Ee *ooh*, ee *ooh*, ee *ooh*.' ' *Way*oh, *way*oh.'

THE NANNY: '*@#%!-wups!' 'Oh, *fine*!' 'To tell the truth . . .' 'Long ago, far away, in a boat out on the sea . . .'

ALL: 'Squeeze, pull and rotate.' 'Load the probe!'

SAME LONG DAY, EVENING, A fortnight out of Christmas and motoring towards Samoa. We have at least five days to go 700-plus nautical miles—if we don't hit whales, a wrong wind (we are too far west for the trades, Nat says) or other disasters. Days are evil, hot and humid. Evenings we all come awake. I was with the kids in their netted bunk and Nathalie was bored, waiting for her ocean productivity readings to download to the computer, so she dropped a wet rope through the hatch onto my face. Very funny. Adam stayed asleep, so the baby and I played a quiet tug-o'-war with her for a while. The baby loves that kind of thing. Adam tends to get too rough, but Simon and I managed a game with him this morning. Tempers are improving with Samoa to look forward to.

Food is odd. We've emptied one water tank and are finishing the good-tasting water from the *Tullymore*, the only other yacht moored off Christmas Island. The *Tullymore* was a lovely three-masted schooner, taking a ritual canoe to Rarotonga, to a Cook Islands cultural festival that we are going to miss. Polynesian dancing, feasting, the works. A little tourism would have been good for the soul about now.

Adam had his moment of glory when the *Tullymore* sent ashore a boatload of kids bound for the Kiritimati airport and home.

Nat and I were already stuck ashore because of the wind. There was just no way *Cachalot's* inflatable dinghy would have made it to shore through that surf. The *Tullymore* tried, though. She had a motorized wooden dinghy, almost a longboat, and a bunch of kids who had been having the bonding experience of crewing at sea. They were due to fly home before the *Tullymore* sailed on to Rarotonga.

The calmer, bay side of Kiritimati was protected by a stiff current and standing wave at the mouth of a shallow harbor that looped behind the island. *Tully* had anchored out by *Cachalot*, not daring to negotiate the tricky maze of army junk in the harbor. The bottom of the bay was a clear, shifting gridwork of sandy channels and rusting hulks and the swallow flight of platter-sized sea turtles darting through eelgrass. Lovely and treacherous. Even the fishermen refused to go out in the heavy winds that bounced the two yachts around just offshore. *Tullymore's* longboat (complete with kids) flipped in the channel where that long cresting wave held its permanent menacing curl, just behind a rip that raced down the outer, ocean side of the island. Cerberus guarding Hades.

From shore, Nathalie and I were only aware that the fishermen were suddenly swinging into boats that had been moored for the duration of the storm. Their wooden dinghies looked far less seaworthy than the fancy longboat, but the men steering were clearly practiced and familiar with the dangers of their guardian current. They navigated it like surfies at a barbecue and caught up every one of the floundering, frightened teenagers—and even some of their gear. From shore we saw some of the action and followed the rest at Tek's grocery store on his VHF, translated by Tek himself. His eldest daughter brought everyone endless cups of steaming coconut-sap tea (to help us sweat and feel cool in the muggy air), and we sat on wooden benches along the corrugated metal walls, our feet on cool woven mats, while people filtered in and out to drink tea and hear the news. We were all terribly proud of the fishermen. CW told us later that no one had been above decks—neither on *Tullymore* nor *Cachalot*—except Adam, who had called the alert by telling his dada that the longboat had gone over in the waves.

I'M WRITING UNDER MOONLIGHT. I have danced myself to a standstill but don't want to turn on the artificial light and pollute the evening. A squall is up ahead, and warm blasts of air keep hitting me like serpent's breath. Nights are the best by far. My days a misery, my nights a wonder, and me in limbo. As usual.

Day 44

SIMON SAYS: *MORE SEA. Our self-steering gear, Clarence, carked it today, and while I was helping nut out how to fix it (the usual no. 8 fencing-wire job), we managed to drop another piece over the side. Managed a repair with maximum effort. We were ruddy stressed because it means constant hands-on steering without the wee bastard. If you duck below to do the listen for whales, the ship wanders off course and you spend the next ten minutes shifting back and adjusting sails. Bang-on fun.*

The heat puts everyone's nerves on edge. The captain put the hard work out that we've got only twenty gallons of

water left, so go easy. We always go easy, so I don't know
how we're meant to cut down. Reckon we could stop in the
Tokelau Islands if we need to. Feeling stonkered, so off to
bed.

Day 45

TO CONTINUE THE TYPICAL DAY: after strapping the
baby in her chair, I go to the galley and get her Cheerios or
mush or whatever I can find. Sometimes I make tea for
whoever is on watch. When we are with whales, people get
up fast, Captain first. If Simon is on watch, Adam jumps on
him and pummels him mercilessly while I feed, clean, diaper
and slime (slop sunblock on) the baby. Her hat ties on last,
like the petals on a slightly greasy flower. Then breakfast for
Adam and me, if I can stomach it by then. Often Nathalie,
our food maven, gets up and makes us something. By the
time the baby is harnessed and ready to brave the bow,
Simon has been up there for some time, despite his 3 to 6
a.m. watch. He's taking photographs and watching in the
slicks—the whale's footprints—for bits of skin or squid or
shit to scoop up in his long-handled net. Really one of us
should be helping with the nets. If the baby lets me, I lend a
hand, but often she's too wriggly. By 7:30 or 8 a.m. CW has
crawled out of her bunk, looking less than pleased to see
daylight. The captain is driving (we motor after the whales
and it really is more like driving than steering), or if he's
been on watch, then sometime around 9 a.m. he'll take the
baby in for her nap while Nathalie steers. CW is usually

below on the hydrophones by then, recording codas as they occur. We've got a dilly of a whale out there today. I got on the phones early and called CW to hear. Our whale was *arf-arf*ing like a seal barking. 'So much for the theories of sperm-whale clicks,' says CW.

Simon hands down a petri dish through the bow hatch. It is full of black tissue-papery whale skin. They shed constantly. I complain that I don't properly know what to do with it, so he comes down and shows me once again how to pour salt water over the skin and separate the clump delicately with two sets of tweezers, then pick it up—while it instantly re-clumps—and dump it into a buffer solution. Then we write the boat's position and the date, ID number and time on waterproof paper and put them inside a plastic container to store with the skin. The same information is also written on the outside, and again in a log marked 'Skin' on one side of its pages and 'Shit' on the other. (Adam loves it when he spots the whale poop first and is allowed to yell 'SHIT!' from the bow.) We also write in the log whether the skin sample can be correlated to an identifying photograph of a tail fluke or not. If I'm still child-free, I go up on deck again—unless more skin is forthcoming—and usually take over the photographing. If not, there is always netting, very occasionally steering, and often I relieve CW on the headphones and record whale talk.

CW's biggest complaint is the impossibility of coordinating what she hears—hunched below with the delicate recording equipment—with what the others see

80

going on with the whales up top. Sometimes the whales coda sub-surface, but in any case, CW constantly yells up—or I do—to ask how many whales, what direction, and what they are up to; side fluking, for instance, seems to go along with creaking. Our last day on whales they were spy-hopping, rolling, rubbing bellies (two males, the captain said), breaching, lobtailing; one male even rolled on his back and showed us his white-and-black speckled jaw. I got an open-jaw chin breach on film. The males are distinctive because of their size: large. The male's rostrum (schnoz) is a third to half the body length and very bulbous. Their backs are knobby with a ridged dorsal and tail. Sometimes they are so bumpy, it looks like the ridges on a dragon's back sliding through the waves.

Sperm whales have a primitive, Stone Age look. They don't sing like humpbacks or chirp like dolphins. The females do regular metronome clicks, one and a half to three seconds apart; the males make five to ten slower clicks and clanging, metallic-sounding creaks like the doors on a haunted house. These make up the codas, the uneven or tightly patterned phrases that stand out from the rest of the sounds and are very individual. Communication? Personal signature? Group dialect (one of this expedition's many subjects of study)? All of the above? I'm still reading CW's thesis and will go on to the other articles afterwards. Reading science papers is slow going during these busy days. We continue to follow the old whalers' routes, look at population, and listen to coda differences between each group. Our whales seem to form smaller, discrete clusters and then come back together again. Much as we do.

And so it goes. Sometimes I jump in the water for fifteen minutes when *Cachalot* heaves to for Nathalie to do her ocean productivity tests. She also does something with the sonar that she says she doesn't completely understand, but since the computer never seems to work properly, it probably doesn't matter. Sometimes the whales spy-hop near us, lifting their chins above the waves to take a good look at their watchers. Occasionally someone jumps overboard to try to see them underwater. The visibility is usually not good enough.

By mid-afternoon I'm happy to retreat into the bowels of the boat and out of the sun—if I can. If someone else is tired of the sun and willing to take the kids, I swap jobs: rarely steering; often photographing; collecting and processing skin samples; recording and then writing up the usual hourly log to record position, boat speed, wind speed and direction, air and water temperature, mileage and ocean depth (which means pinpointing our position visually on the charts with calipers). All kinds of fun. Then someone has to cook, so if it isn't my turn I'm often up on the bow or up the mast towards the end of the day. Late afternoon I go up the mast for as long as I can, sometimes with CW steering and Nathalie being casual with her bottomless cup of tea and one eye on a net. ('Casual' depends on whether or not we have netted plenty of sloughed whale skin.) Nat is the only person I know who will down cup after cup of hot tea in egg-frying weather. She says it kills the taste of the tank water. She drinks an amazing amount of water for a small person. Says it keeps her healthy.

Sunset and dinner come together back in the cockpit. Hopefully we are near enough to the whales that we don't have to chase after them right away while we switch from visual tracking to following them with the directional hydrophone as the sky darkens.

Adam had another temper tantrum last night. When his mom put him to bed, he was yelling, 'My mom's too much for me!' and 'Dada, I need you badly!' We were all trying not to laugh. CW thinks he got the first line from *The Elephant's Child*. He has a pretty good vocabulary for a five-year-old and has some German as well from his mother. He pronounces 'very' as 'werry', and says, 'Thank you. It was werry, werry nice,' ever so politely, after even the most heinous dinner. He does have charm, that kid. And the more I lose my cool with him, the more stubborn he gets. My authority with him lasted not at all. Simon is good with him, but Adam doesn't know when to quit and has physically hurt us all now and then. Saintly Simon has definitely become more acerbic and occasionally warrants his new nickname, Saintly-Simon-the-Sometimes-Simply-Sadist.

Day 46

SIMON SAYS: *DAWN WATCH CAME UP IN Technicolor along with the wee sprogs, who were surprisingly good-natured for the early a.m. Otherwise, all is normal except for a couple of sudden, massive downpours. We collected water* from the canopy runoff and added it to our dwindling supplies. Ended up with several gallons in the jerry cans. Still so bloody hot, both air and water, but with an occasional choice breeze we're rattling along at seven to eight knots. Somehow, Samoa looks farther and farther away, despite all efforts to the contrary. Had the usual dinner of lentils and rice. Can't wait to get back to NZ, see my mates, see how the seabird project is going. I can't throw the feeling I lack a proper home. Can't stop dreaming.

Day 47

I'M A BASKET CASE.

Day 48

SIMON SAYS: *ANOTHER MISERABLY HOT day. Except for the occasional rain cloud it's ruddy unbearable. Air temp at 31 degrees and water at 29 degrees Celsius. We collected more rain off the deck and canopy. Managed to get quite a bit. The water crisis gets more desperate, but the rain catch today will help. Seem to be ignoring whales. Reckon we heard three today and tried to follow one but couldn't sort out the bearing. We haven't got enough patience, water or food to comfortably spend even a few days following a whale. Drinking water is the limiting factor. Course 150 degrees to avoid hitting Tokelau last night. Not worth stopping because of strong winds, our Captain says.*

Day 49

STILL SAMOA-BOUND. WE ARE running out of water.
For food, we are down to lentils, lentils and more lentils.
Lentils cooked in seawater, lentils with lentils, dry lentils.
Methane city.

Two more ships passed in the night. It seemed like
mine would be the watch from hell. It was squally when
Nathalie woke me with the inevitable cup of tea. She told me
to pull in the genoa and motor if things got too rough. When
I did, the self-steering wouldn't work right, and I knocked
Clarence the self-steerer's chain off. I got Nat before she fell
asleep but had to wake the captain after all, as she couldn't
fix it either (I had twisted it around 300 degrees or so). The
captain came up and fixed Clarence—again—and by then
there were lights on the horizon.

I would have sweated bullets up there by myself, but
the captain stayed above decks with me for my entire 3 to 6
a.m. watch. He explained how one should take a bearing on
the boat and then check that bearing several minutes later. If
the bearing hasn't changed, then you know the boat is
coming towards you. Also, the forward white light tends to
be lower than the aft running light, and as soon as they get
close enough to see colors, then you can make out the right
green, left red running-lights. I did a hydrophone listen for
the whales (half an hour late) and could hear the other boats
*shush-shush*ing through the water, like the engine noises
from the movie *Das Boot*. It was eerie, as the night became
paler, to see the two stars I was watching so anxiously turn

85

into the huge grey hulls of a cargo ship and possibly a Japanese fishing boat. No ships for weeks, and then two within two nautical miles of each other. I think that's the first real talk I've had with the captain.

Heard the whale and then, thankfully—finally— Samoa on the VHF.

THE CAPTAIN IS SITTING IN the cockpit just now telling Simon a story about a researcher back home who was trying to prove that baleen whales have sonar by tying a rope to the tail of a humpback that had gotten caught in a fishing weir. He blindfolded it somehow and tried to make it go through a maze of bamboo poles he had set up. It didn't work. Poor scared whale just ploughed straight through the lot. Evidently, the same researcher then tried to set up an experiment to show that whales navigate using some kind of telepathic communication with their barnacles.

The other story the captain tells that I like is the one about the dead whale on the beach. He says he saw the film footage at a conference, but the story already has the feel of urban legend. Some town's road crew couldn't figure out how to get rid of the whale, so they decided to blow it up with dynamite. That way, the seagulls could carry it away in smaller chunks. It seems the crew had a lot of spectators, one with a camera, and the way the captain described it, there was this sort of *crump*! as the dynamite blew, the crowd went, 'Ah!' and then the cries changed more to, 'Argh!' The camera person yelled, 'Oh my god!' and fifty- to one-hundred-pound chunks of blubber started splatting down through the air. A VW Beetle some distance away got completely squashed by a huge, smelly chunk of blown-up whale. It's a legend now. Revenge of the squashalot.

THE PROBLEM ABOARDSHIPS IS THE extremes. There is the moonlight on the water, there is the nausea in the morning. After nine more months of this I could have my very own bundle of joy and drool. Write, write, write. If I didn't have that, I'd go mad.

Christmas Island

I THINK THE STORY I most want to talk about Kiritimati is the story of Father Christmas. Nathalie and I had been staying at the Catholic mission, eating at Perry and Erena's, out of various people's household stores, and occasionally making the long trek out towards Banana for a shower.

Mostly we walked on the beaches, talking to people. That first windy day, after waving my arms futilely at *Cachalot* for the better part of the morning, I gave up and went for a walk on the calmer bay side of the island. I came across one of Erena's daughters making a fire on the beach. She called, 'Ko na mauri! Ko uara?' and invited me to join her, showing me some fish roasting in a small fire pit she'd dug in the sand. She started to feed me, as her mother had the night before, and I decided that was not on. I knew we were being treated as honorary males. I wanted to respect other customs but not at the expense of my own beliefs.

'I won't eat if you don't,' I said.

She looked angry. 'No, you eat,' she said.

'I will if you will . . .'

'Oh!' Frustration. Then, 'Well then, you will be a kid for today!' she announced and squatted down to eat with me. We'd been completely alone under a line of coconut trees on the beach, not a roof in sight, but suddenly we were surrounded by young people. Everyone grabbed at the fish without regard for ranking.

They laughed at my hesitation over the fish heads. Several of the older boys brought out huge machetes and

88

lopped the tops off green coconuts for us to drink. I was an oddity but no longer untouchable, and they screamed with laughter when I tried to climb the coconut tree to see where they collected the sap for toddy. I got to the edge of the leaves and lost my nerve, but it was close enough to see the Coke bottles tapped in at the base of the giant green fronds.

The wedge steps cut in the trunk were slippery and green with mildew, but when I slid, several hands placed themselves under my instep and on the backs of my legs to help me down.

The boys got bored finally and drifted away while I sat talking with Erena's daughter. A flock of tiny children had just milled past, gleaning every last scrap of leftover food as they went. She had paid special attention to one tiny boy.

'Is he yours?' I asked sleepily, thinking of the wall of pictures in Erena's house, where she had proudly pointed out her own children, Perry's children, and Perry's children by her best friend.

'Of *course* not!' the girl said quickly. 'I am going to school next year on the mainland [Solomon Islands]. I have no husband.'

'Do you have a boyfriend?' I asked.

'Yes,' she giggled. 'He is on the mainland now. That little boy,' and her face softened, 'he is one who had no one, so my auntie took him into her house.'

'What usually happens to children who have no one?' I asked.

'There is always room for children,' she shrugged, and we scraped sand over the little fire.

That night we watched a video at Perry and Erena's house. It was a disorienting experience. They owned one of three televisions on the island, keeping this treasure safe in their open-sided tin-roofed hut that seemed to grow out of its cement pad. Inside, a huge bed covered in mosquito netting dominated the middle of the room. The woven back wall was entirely covered in photographs, and an ancient Pepsi icebox in one corner served as TV stand and warm Coke and Fanta dispenser. In that tropical paradise of coconut and rich reef fishes we watched Arnold Schwarzenegger go to Mars in *Total Recall.*

There had been only Erena, Perry, Nathalie, Fred and I in the room to begin with, but midway through the movie I became aware of an almost subliminal rustling and looked away from the bright screen. The entire floor of the house was carpeted with small, silent children. Until my eyes adjusted, I couldn't see anything but a shifting darkness that resolved into small, intent heads turned like flowers towards the light of the television. There was not an inch of floor space left. Perry knew they were there, or assumed it, since his eyes never left the TV, but while passively allowing the most violent and bloody gore on the screen, he grumbled and fast-forwarded through every love scene.

Which brings me back, finally, to the church. There was a Protestant mission on the island as well as a Catholic church. The two enjoyed a fairly friendly but determined competition for the souls of the people. Each churchyard had a huge, roofed gathering area called a *mwaneaba*, with a cement floor that we were told was where the men came to sleep when their wives kicked them out. Since this seemed a common occurrence, we asked why.

'Drink,' we were told. 'They come here when they go home drunk and she says, "Get lost!"'

Nathalie was the first to notice we were being closely watched in our daily perambulations around the island. We'd had such a warm reception from so many people, it never occurred to us that we were causing confusion as well. It is all very well to be treated as honorary males, but no one really knew what we were doing there or why two women were staying at the Catholic mission. Suddenly, it seemed every time we went near the building where we slept, a little man in a kind of ragged burlap toga and sandals appeared and gave us the evil eye. Fred told us he was an acolyte of the church. Fred thought maybe it was time we were going. We didn't really have much choice. We ignored the little man, and Fred, and stayed.

The night the winds died down; the Catholic Father came home. Fred was furious that we were still there. We had made an effort and cleaned the section of the house where we had stayed but felt very shy about meeting the man who had been our unknowing host, especially given the obvious anxiety over our presence. The Father turned out to be a lovely man. Like Nathalie he was Swiss–French, just returning from a long visit home. He greeted Nathalie like a long-lost relative and insisted that we join him for his welcome-home ceremony that evening. We agreed, then flew out the door to see what food we could buy for the boat. It was obvious we'd be going back aboard the next day. We hitched to the old barracks, mid-island, and even farther out to the airport, where canned supplies were flown in by the government. At each place we were told, 'No, we have nothing to sell you.' They needed what few supplies came in for themselves. We did score a welcome block of cheese and a few tins of Spam (which CW gave away later to another boat).

We went and found Erena. I asked if I could pay her kids to fill some sacks with coconuts and she laughed at me, sending her children off on our errands for free. Then she and I stole into the neighbor's yard to spy out one of the huge, kernelled pandanus fruit, as big as my torso, for her sons to steal later from the tree.

'Pandanus are the toes of Nei Tituabine,' Erena whispered, giggling. 'Mother of the plants. When she died, her head sprouted into a coconut palm, and her feet grew the pandanus.' (How I wish now I could have told her what a wallop those toes packed aboardships.)

We went next to a fisherman's house and saw piles of different species of dried fish being distributed to the neighbors. Erena helped us select a sackful for the boat. Tek, who managed the biggest store in London Town—and who monitored the big ship-to-shore radio that had organized the longboat passengers' rescue mission—insisted we take, as a gift, two wine bottles filled with coconut sap that had been boiled down to the consistency of molasses and tasted rich and coconut-sweet.

We made it back to the mission late, just after dark. All the lights were off in the building, but there was plenty of noise coming from the roofed patio out in the yard where the drunken husbands were meant to sleep. We both felt so shy we almost didn't go over, but for politeness' sake we thought we ought at least to say hello.

It was a sight. The Father was in the middle of the huge floor, squatting cross-legged like a white-haired Buddha covered in flowers. He had ropes of white flowers in his hair and around his neck and a little tray of food sitting next to him.

A good six meters away a circle of men sat on mats staring at him. They also had food trays. Behind them lounged the women, chatting to one another and seemingly paying little attention to the proceedings. They had no food.

The Father spotted us at the edge of the floor before we had time to flee.

He called us over, right into the middle of all the staring faces.

'Sit with me here,' Nathalie translated for him. 'I'm lonely in the middle.'

So we sat with him and shared his food, much to the consternation of the little goblin-faced acolyte who had given us the evil eye for days. The acolyte suddenly stood up and everyone stopped eating to listen.

'Who are these women?' he asked abruptly, and the Father chuckled as he translated for us.

The Father took the circlet of flowers off his hair and placed them on Nathalie's head, then he took the rope of flowers from his neck and placed them around my neck.

When I protested, he told me, through Nathalie, that he felt silly in flowers.

'This woman,' the Father pointed at Nathalie, 'is my countrywoman. She comes from a town near my home, where I have been travelling these six months. I want you all to welcome her into your hearts and homes.'

The acolyte was not pleased, but I got the impression that the hospitality we had already received would be nothing compared with what it would have been, if only we could have stayed. The Father had handed us London Town. The little acolyte stood up again.

'When is the Pope coming to visit us?'

The Father answered diplomatically. And so it went: he translated for us, and Nathalie translated for me, as each man got up and welcomed the Father home, asked about his trip, and asked him one religious question.

The food on the tray was excellent: baked meats wrapped in leaves, fried flat breads and tree-ripe fruit. Being herself, Nathalie was taking her time eating. The third time the Father asked her if she'd had enough to eat, and she had replied again with her typical, 'Oh, no! No point rushing good food!', I noticed something and punched her on the arm. When each tray around the circle was about half empty it was being pushed back to where the women were sitting. A certain group was eyeing our tray critically as its contents fast disappeared down Nathalie's gullet. She turned scarlet.

I took the tray back to the women at the edge of the group, dying to get out of the middle of the circle, and the family sharing the mat took my hands and asked me to stay.

One of the women spoke English, as did many of the adults on the island, and she translated some of what was going on. Nathalie glared at me from the center of the room where I had abandoned her.

'Thank you for joining us,' the woman said. 'You do us a favor by bringing more people into the Joan of Arc club.'

I had joined the club. Each mat turned out to belong to a different club, all competing to have the most people in attendance. Joan of Arc was shy a few members: someone was drunk, someone was celebrating a new baby, someone else was just lazy, they told me. I was now an honorary member.

We kept the sweet-smelling flower leis for weeks, swinging from *Cachalot's* cabin roof.

Day 50 - 52

SIMON SAYS: *OUR WATER TANKS ARE DRY. The heat continues, and we have well over 200 nautical miles to Pago Pago and eight gallons of rainwater left in the jerry cans. Got the guts that strict rationing will be enforced tomorrow if we don't all ruddy well behave. We are sailing past whales because we can't afford to stop now. No water, no whales. Nathalie is saying, 'I told you so.' The temp is well over thirty degrees Celsius, with little wind. The whole world seems to be moving slower than a whingeing Pom.*

Day 51

AT 5:30 A.M., MY THERMOMETER READ 110°Fahrenheit. Every time I move a finger, I break out in a sweat. Finally a bit of wind so the genoa is up. Thank God, a bit of shade. We motored all last night, and the fumes were starting to give the baby a hack. Water is down to the few remaining gallons in our jerry cans. Mutinous thoughts are rampant.

Nathalie is irate about the food and water situation on board. In reaction to the captain asking people to cut down on water use, she has upped hers. More tea, and full cups to brush her teeth with. She is seriously pissed off. To her, water is the thing you don't stint on in stinking hot weather. Cooking plain lentils (with no garlic!) in seawater is pretty yuck. We do have lentils. And lentils, and did I forget to mention LENTILS?

96

This 360-degree horizon makes you want to get somewhere . . .

Day 52

SIMON SAYS: *NOT A SAUSAGE IN SIGHT on the horizon. Everyone is tense. Nat, the Yank and I have been motor-sailing every opportunity at max revs. The captain doesn't quite approve, but doesn't say no. Meals lately have been plain as an Ocker's bride. Despite everything, I've told the Captain I'll stay aboard after New Zealand. But every night I dream of home.*

> Experience is that marvelous thing that enables you to recognize a mistake when you make it again.
>
> —F. P. Jones

5.
Boat Dreamings

Old Dreams: Hunger Fish

Never let the truth get in the way of a good story.
—Simon

SIMON'S BEST MATE, TIMMY, HAD two daddies, Simon told us one night over tea, eyeing his mixed audience of one American, one Swiss French, one Brit–Canadian, one German American, and a new generation holding passports from at least three of those countries. One daddy was named Square, Simon said, because he was so cool. The other one was called 'That *Pee-Ahr-Eye-See-Kay*' by Timmy's mum (but that's another story). Square looked like Elvis. He was one big rough daddy from the Nga Puhi tribe, the most warlike in New Zealand, sometimes called Rat-eaters, Simon grinned.

You Americans and Commonwealth types don't know it, he said, but the Maori are one of the First Peoples who actually kicked butt when the English colonists tried to take over their islands. They named the English Pakeha, or Pale Fairy, which the English took as a compliment, but might not have been. Puha was a kind of local spinach that Timmy had to eat when he was young, because it had lots of iron in it. That was because the family never had red meat to eat, only the fish they caught and the puha they picked by the side of the road.

There is an old song in New Zealand called 'Puha and Pakeha', about stewing up a nice Pakeha with a mess of greens. That's pretty much what the Maori thought of the

English colonists, Simon said.

The colonists had their own song that went:

> No moa, no moa, in old Ao-tea-roa,
> Can't get 'em, they've 'et 'em,
> They've gone and there ain't no moa!
> —W. Chamberlain

That was the Pakeha complaining about the Maori having eaten all the giant native birds, which is why everyone was left with only fish to eat (and sheep, but that's another story too). So you get the idea that there is a bit of tension between Maori and Pakeha, and that food (kai) is what is at the bottom half of most disputes.

Timmy was always hungry. Timmy's three stepbrothers, two half-siblings and visiting cousins were always hungry. Square spent his time getting kai moana, food from the ocean, to feed his hungry family. Timmy's mum was Pakeha and Square was Maori, so already you get the idea that food was at the bottom half of most of their disputes, too.

One day Timmy's mum said to her handsome husband, 'Husband, will you get up off your hairy backside and get us some bloody fish for tonight's tea?'

And her husband answered lovingly, 'Get stuffed, you old cow,' but he pulled out their tin dinghy—called the tinny—stuck a motor on it and started to haul it down to the water.

'Oi!' said his Delicate Flower. 'Take the blasted

102

ankle-biters with you.' But nary an ankle nosher was to be found except young Tim. He was lost in a book of pictures showing brave, blood-drenched heroes rescuing impossibly buxom wenches from toothy monsters of the deep.

'That Pakeha boy of yours don't know from fish,' said Square.

'Takim ennyway,' said his sweet-tongued spouse. 'Always gotiz nose in some book,' she grumbled, already planning for soup and crackers in case they came back empty-handed. And so it was that Timmy went on his first fishing trip with his stepdaddy, Square.

Now there are many ways to fish. There is fishing when the boat rocks you to sleep in the sun and waves while the snapper and blue cod nibble around the edges of your bait. There is the sort when you throw a round net and let weights drop it into a jellyfish cup shape, pulling the opening shut when you think the blue cod and the snapper aren't noticing. Or there's the sort of fishing you do when you know you'll catch blue blazes from your mate if you don't bring back something, and if that's true, you might as well gobsmack her completely with something really impressive. Something bigger, something tastier, something that might try to taste you back. The biggest, granddaddiest, most monster/taniwha hapuka that you can catch. For that, you need an extra-strong line.

This is what Square told Timmy as they motored out beyond the sandbanks. And then, there was the matter of bait. 'Cause there was nothing, not a blessed thing, that a giant hapuka loved more than genuine, puha-fed Pakeha.

'Lucky for us,' said Square, 'we got one aboard.'

Now, Timmy had just been taught to swim the summer before, by his big stepbrother Elliot who threw him in the surf and dragged him backward by the heels until he got it right. So he knew he could do it. But Square had in mind tying the fishing line around Tim's middle, so he could haul both boy and fish into the boat should the hapuka deign to nibble his toes. Timmy wasn't sure he liked that idea. He wanted there to be a hook. The only really big hook on the boat was the one Square wore around his neck.

'Can't give you that, boy,' Square said. 'That hook holds me mana.'

And by that, Simon told his audience, Square meant something like his soul. The hook had been given him by his great-grandmother, and her mother's mother before her. It was made of pounamu, and it was Square's most precious treasure, his taonga.

But as Square looked at the boy making ready to fling himself off the stern of the tinny, he changed his mind.

'Nah, I was only jokin', mate,' he said. And together they took the thick rope that usually tied up the tinny and knotted the giant greenstone hook into the end of it, so that it could turn and shine in the water. Square thought the hook alone would be enough for any hapuka, and he was willing to admit that a small hapuka would do just fine. But at the last moment Timmy grabbed the hook and jumped overboard.

''E's a good boy,' muttered Square, and settled down for a nap in the sun.

104

AND WHILE SQUARE SLEPT, THIS is what happened to young Timmy. First, he splashed into the water and got wet. Then he surfed behind the tinny for a while, hanging on to the rope, yelling and feeling fine. Then the tinny stopped moving with the current, and the great weight of the massive greenstone hook began to take the rope slowly down, into the pale blue water of the bay.

Timmy hung on to that hook. He knew Daddy's magic was in it, and he wasn't about to let go. Down into the deep, past the red snapper and the blue cod still nibbling at the smaller trailing lines, past the surprised eels and the aggrieved kina raising their spines. Down into the home of the biggest granddaddy hapuka.

When he hit bottom, Timmy knew he was in the lair of a true taniwha—the oldest monster—because he didn't even need to breathe.

He wasn't sure he could.

Something to know about hapuka: even the little ones have projectile mouths. They can throw their lips ahead of their bodies without having to budge. These lips have little serrated edges that grab hold and help yank in whatever the sheer suction can't handle. What Timmy thought was a strange, seaweed-colored cave was really the open mouth of the monster hapuka, all set about with ragged edges. It hadn't moved yet, it hadn't sucked him in, but a big rolling eye beside the mouth cavern had spotted the flashing green hook, and the little pale Pakeha riding it.

No one really wants to catch a taniwha. A taniwha is a force of nature, far more likely to catch you than contrariwise. Timmy found that out when the hapuka opened its big gill slits and the cave turned into giant lips that reached out, a whirlpool of water sucking him in and in and . . .

. . . turning end over end he . . .

. . . the rope in his hand it . . .

. . . flashing hook getting away that . . .

. . . a solid red bar of breathing gill, sweeping oxygen over him, a handhold . . .

. . . a hookhold . . .

. . . the whirlpool subsided. Timmy had hooked the hapuka in the gills, was still hanging on.

The grandfather taniwha spoke to him. It had a magic greenstone hook from the grandmother ancestors in its gills, a small Pakeha stuck alongside like a mite. It spoke to him.

'Whatchu want, boy?'

'Want a big hapuka feed for my family,' whispered Timmy.

Hapuka laughed. Almost dislodged the hook. Timmy held on.

'Think you gonna eat this kai, boy?'

'No sir.' Timmy cleared his throat. 'Might as well eat an elephant, sir.'

Hapuka didn't seem to know *elephant.*

'Big, eh?'

'Too big, but,' said the boy.

'Think I should give a Pakeha boy me own children to eat?'

'You have a lot of children, taniwha, and this

greenstone's got my daddy's mana in it. You'd feed your children's children, eh?'

Hapuka looked puzzled as a cross-eyed pollywog.

'Got me there, boy. Things changing up in the air world, I reckon. Whatchu give me, I feed your family this time?'

'I'll take this old stone out of your gills,' Timmy said.

'What else?' laughed the monster.

'I'll tell you a story.'

'Ho!' said the hapuka and was quiet for a heartbeat. 'About a hapuka?'

'Okay,' said Timmy, 'about a hapuka.'

SQUARE OPENED HIS EYES TO look at his wife's son, who was sitting in the boat grinning at him, a fish across his lap that spanned the tinny from side to side. Square's greenstone fishhook flashed around his neck.

'Whatchu got there, son?' the man said, grinning back.

'Got me a wee little hapuka for a family feed.'

'Just a wee one, I see.'

'Yes, he's only wee.'

'That's my boy,' the man said, 'Can tell a story, too.' And he turned the boat homeward towards the Queen of his Nights, the Flower of his Existence, and Timmy and his daddy kept, for perhaps the first time, a full and companionable silence.

And if it didn't happen in just that way, it should have.

107

IT WAS AFTERWARDS, SIMON SAID, that his mate Timmy changed his name to Temuera. Square told Simon that the name sounded an awful lot like a Maori word that means either a tough, pale swamp blossom or the burned buttocks of a Maori princess

—but that's another story.

New Dreams: Raisons d'être

> Nothing of him that doth fade,
> But doth suffer a sea-change
> Into something rich and strange.
> —Shakespeare, *The Tempest*

WHY ARE WE HERE? WHERE are we going?

Simon says he wants to be an arbiter one day between research scientists and wildlife managers. He wants to help fix some old arguments. He dreams of his broken family in sleepy grays. Where are the whales in that?

I say I want to write about the sciences for lay people. I like knowing how things work. I want to see the world and tell stories. But I dream of love and sun-warmed apricots in hopeful yellow orange. Where are the whales in that?

The Captain's Wife wants to help save things—the whales, her family—and to make her mark. She always dreamed of marrying a biologist, she says, but now she dreams in dry earth browns. Where are the whales in that?

We observe the captain contributing to the body of scientific knowledge. His eyes reflect dreams of flat, sun-seared blue. It has everything to do with whales.

Nathalie dreams of blood-red steak. We hope there are no whales in that.

And the children?

The children dream of us.

Dreaming Up Stories: The Misremembered

> 'I,' said the bug,
> 'Am a sea-going tug.
> Am I headed for land, do you think?'
> —John Ciardi, *I Met a Man*

'SHALL I TELL YOU THE story of The Little Canadian Who Swallowed the Sea?'

'With monsters?'

'There are always monsters.'

'All right then.'

'There was a little boy, who sailed with his family around the world.'

'And his name was Adam!'

'That's right. Adam had an extraordinary ability. He could lean down, like so, and drink up all the water in the ocean, and hold it with his cheeks puffed out to here.'

'Why did he drink up all the ocean?'

'His family was often hungry, and when Adam drank up the water, they would walk out onto the ocean floor and collect just enough fish to eat and bring them back to their boat. Then Adam would go, *PHPPHPHPHPHPHPthp!* And with a sound like a giant raspberry, he would let all the water there was flow back into the ocean, covering up its treasures again.'

'And did they bring back the fish and treasure to *Cachalot?*'

110

'No, they played with the treasure, sometimes long enough that Adam had trouble holding the ocean in, because it really is tough to keep your cheeks puffed up like a chipmunk for so long. They left the treasure where it belonged, only taking just enough fish for a lovely evening feed as the sun went down.'

'Don't forget the monsters.'

'One day, some other boats were nearby when Adam drank up the sea, and those people ran down to the ocean floor and collected some fish as well.'

'And they stole the treasure?'

'Pretty much, because soon everyone heard about it, and every evening when Adam leaned over to drink up the whole ocean, a flotilla of fishing boats gathered around, and everyone on board ran down to harvest the fish in huge baskets. They weren't taking just enough fish to eat; they were getting greedy and taking all the fish there were.'

'Were they the monsters?'

'I really don't know. But one day, Adam had to hold the water back for a long, long time. He could see that there were still people wandering around on the ocean floor, searching for more and more fish, but going farther and farther away, because there weren't many fish left nearby. He was in an agony to let the ocean flow back into its bed, and he waved wildly for the people to hurry back to their boats.'

'I would let all the water go back! *PHPHPHPHPHP Hththpt!*'

'And so he did. Finally, he could hold it in no more, and the ocean came rumbling, and the ocean came roaring. And the ocean went *PHPHPHththpt!* Back into its bed with a sound like someone blowing a giant raspberry.'

'And were all the people drownded?'

'That was the strange thing. Adam's family, and a few people left behind in the other boats, were watching the water sadly, wondering what had happened to the fishermen with their baskets of fish, and they heard a noise like a big, shushing *poooh*! Then they heard another, and another *poooh*! And they saw something that looked like huge baskets being pushed through the water, chasing after the fish.'

'It was whales!'

'Yes. The people left behind on the ocean floor had all turned into baleen whales, and they were still chasing the fish around with their huge collecting baskets. But you know what? They never, ever again managed to catch more than was just enough to eat. Adam never, ever drank up the sea again. But he did teach his family how to blow some really choice raspberries.'

'Now tell one with a sword!'

Sea Dreams: What the Captain Said

The whale is a mammiferous animal without
hind feet.

—Baron Cuvier, *Moby-Dick*

'SPERM WHALES, *CACHALOT*, ARE MEMBERS of the
odontocete or toothed-whale family. They have an
imperfectly understood sonar system—far more effective
than anything the world's navies have built—and a single,
off-centre blowhole. Males can grow as large as twenty
meters. Unlike baleen whales, such as the humpback whale,
the males are larger than the females and, as adults, spend
most of their time alone in the rich feeding grounds of the
Arctic and Antarctic poles. Because the whalers used to find
one large male with a group of females on their flensing
decks, they assumed the male was a bull who herded his cows.
Recently, our noninvasive research has shown that a big
male may travel long distances to visit the matriarchal
nursery pods at the equator for a mere few hours or days
before continuing on his solitary way.

'A sperm whale at the surface of the sea looks very odd.
Often we see just the top of a long boxy head showing above
water, but that head can be almost a third of the whale's body
length. Sperm whales do not have white patterning on their
tale flukes like the humpback whale. Their skin is
corrugated, their backs—aft of the dorsal fin—lumpy and,
half hidden by waves, they look exactly like enormous, great,
grey, wrinkled dill pickles.'

6.
American Samoa: November

Samoan Sally & the Rusty Can

(Regarding fear, fleeing & fitting in)

> It is generally well known that out of the crews
> of Whaling vessels (American) few ever return
> in the ships on board of which they departed.
> —'Cruise in a Whale Boat', *Moby-Dick*

CACHALOT'S CREW TALKED MOSTLY ABOUT Sally, while hiking through brush so gnarled and intense that walking was as difficult as staggering along on our ever-rocking boat. The three of us had demanded our free time and gotten it, after several days of working on the boat first, readying her for the next step of our voyage. Then we set off to climb Rainmaker, since the Mate had announced that we should climb the highest peak in American Samoa.

The Captain's Wife and I had gotten into a dust-up in our first few hours in harbor, when we docked and found Customs was closed for the weekend, no one allowed to set foot ashore. I was meant to cook that night and begged a bud of garlic off some lounging yachties, describing, a bit dramatically perhaps, our lack of food and water. We'd been cooking in seawater for days, I said—salt, at least, we didn't need. The yachties appeared later with cold sodas, spices, fresh vegetables and a pack of cards, quickly settling in for a visit and a game. CW had a talk with me below decks then, gesturing at the half-empty bottles of lentils and beans, no longer rattling in their cupboards.

'We have enough food left for a Third World country!' she said angrily, probably embarrassed.

'Yes,' I said, feeling grim, and went above to accept the gifts of food. What else was there to say? I asked the others as we set off for Rainmaker, but what we all needed was a topic far removed from boat life, and Sally and her dance at the bar were an easy focus.

I had wanted so badly to stride freely, but each step through the brush required a slash of the borrowed machete, a careful placing of the feet, and tremendous effort to pull oneself up and over and under and around. The white ants were alerted by the Kiwi's passing, angered by the Mate's, and found me to be the perfect slow target for their resentful bites and stings. We hadn't realized until after setting out— and after asking directions twice—that we were meant to apply to the local chiefs for permission to walk on tribal land. But we had no money for presents, and no time for nattering (as the Kiwi put it), so we just went, missing the path and sweating for hours in the muggy heat. Once, we climbed over brush that parted to reveal blue sky beneath, and found we'd climbed a downed tree without noticing.

We stopped at a milky-white stream and lay in it, face down, drinking without worrying too much about the color of the water, because if we didn't drink, we'd die of thirst.

Our experience at the bar the previous evening became the main topic of conversation, taking our thoughts away from the self-imposed struggle. The Mate and I described for the Kiwi—who'd stayed aboard that evening —the four tremendously fat airline pilots who'd sat two tables over, ogling a woman dancing by herself on an otherwise empty floor. She was beautiful—an exotic Grace Kelly, impossibly graceful. She seemed to have few inhibitions, gyrating her body in the middle of the dance floor, hands fluttering like petals, while the rest of the patrons watched from the shadows. The dancer teased the pilots, flipping her short skirt at them, peeking coyly over her shoulder while she padded barefoot into statuesque poses lasting just a heartbeat. She was all golden-brown legs and arse-length black hair.

If four big guys could mill like lemmings, that was what the pilots were doing. When the dancer spun near their table, they'd lean forward with excitement, almost panting until she acknowledged them with a flit or a wiggle. Then they would rear back in horror, surging forward and back like beached whales in surf.

I was surprised when two of the pilots came over to the table I shared with the Mate, both of us clean and showered for the first time in weeks but feeling weatherworn and shabby, one peeling with sunburn, the other stiff and grim, huge glasses glinting in the candlelight. Hardly competition for the main attraction. Nor were we very comfortable talking to strangers, having had none but the boat's company for so long.

The pilots introduced themselves, settling uninvited into the padded bar chairs, blubber rippling. They showed none of the signs of bewildered restraint they'd exhibited towards the dancer. Drinks were ordered.

'So what do you think of Sally there, eh?' asked the

biggest man, leaning too close and jerking his thumb at the dancer still undulating by herself under the lights.

'She's lovely.'

'Maybe. Maybe so.' He sat back, rubbing his stomach idly with one hand, the other going up to touch his hair.

'Why don't you ask her to dance?'

'Not like any Samoan woman I've ever seen,' said the second pilot.

'It bothers you that she's . . . confident?'

'One way of saying it,' said the second man.

'If one could only be sure,' said the first fat man.

'The question is,' the second man said hoarsely, 'is she a woman?'

'*Ai, cojones*,' the Mate muttered.

'Yes, very likely,' the fat men giggled.

'Would either of you like to dance?' the second man leered hopefully at the Mate.

I danced with the bigger of the two pilots. He was courteous and danced well. I found myself putting it on a bit —not for the man, but in solidarity with the dancer, with Sally, who stood laughing at us, barefoot in the middle of the floor, turning round and round to watch.

The next day, while we three walked and talked our tortuous way up the mountain, the Kiwi suddenly announced that any woman as bloody suave as Sally, dancing alone in front of that group of ratbags, would draw fire for sure. She didn't fit the pattern, did she? The men would be shit-scared of her, no matter what her original gender.

'Well,' the Mate said, 'it is interesting, is it not, that

120

even those Old Good Boys never say anything but "she".'

Their comments made me feel more charitable towards my shipmates, even while slapping at the biting ants, wondering if we'd live through another of the Mate's adventures.

We pulled ourselves up out of the streambed into something that looked like a miniature banana plantation. None of the plants were over a few feet high, and the tiny bananas were no larger than our fingers, hanging in little green fists. There were other, taller plants that kept the diminutive plantation in shade. It was easier walking among the bananas, although we had to duck to keep our heads in the clearing under the more tangled canopy overhead. The ground was cool, dark and springy with humus. It felt so good to take longer steps.

Passing over a crest, we found a steep gully cutting down to a stream that angled steeply from the peaks ahead. Opposite was the dense tangle we'd struggled through before, and straight ahead was a slick mudslide that dropped straight over the edge of the gully into another—or the same—milky stream. It was at least a fifteen-meter drop down onto huge flat rocks winking with mica. The Mate's first suggestion was to climb down to the streambed again and follow it up to the peak. That seemed impossible. The fast way forward seemed to mean crossing the mudslide. The soles of my feet hurt just looking at the angle of the slide and the drop beside it. There were several dead tree-fern stumps sticking out of the mud halfway across, otherwise the mud looked liquefied and smooth, without a single handhold.

The Kiwi went first, trekking across on hands and knees. The Mate scrambled across next, joining him in the roots of a flattened tree on the other side. I just stood and stared after them. My backpack was a heavy weight hauling me back. The surface underfoot was untrustworthy.

'Get *stuffed*!' I yelled, frustrated, and got catcalls back from the other two, balanced in a huddle on the tangled tree roots across the slip. It didn't look that much better on their side. I hate doing things that go against instinct. I wanted desperately to be back in the tangle of comfortable trees and vines, providing so many things to hold on to. A first tentative step forward squelched sideways and down.

Keep moving, I told myself, and you can keep ahead of the sideways slip. But when the ground moved under me, I stopped in panic, imagining the slow drift towards the drop.

I scrambled forward another few steps then fell, one arm disappearing into mud up to my armpit. The mud slipped sickeningly sideways again, taking me with it until my knee hooked around one of the dead tree-fern stumps and I stopped.

I caught my breath but couldn't move forwards again. The whole slip felt ready to give way. I felt pinned to the mud by fear.

'You rat bastards!' I yelled again, trying to get angry, to move. My crewmates called encouragement. The Kiwi sounded scared, but the Mate was laughing.

'I'm going to leave behind your damned rum!' I yelled back.

'Time to keep going,' the Mate called, sounding calm

and cheerful. 'Just a bit more—time to move now.'

Pushing with the arm sunk in mud, straightening the leg that wasn't hooked around the fern stump, the pack weighing me down, was like a struggle in a slow-motion dream. I was a bug drowning in treacle. I hated to leave that stump. I couldn't remember afterwards exactly how I got across, but it was a mad scramble through moving mud and silt that seemed determined to carry solid bodies over the drop. When I finally reached the oasis of the tree roots, there was barely room for one more. I could see down through the roots and again saw sky beneath our feet. There was nowhere to go but up into the thick canopy of rainforest.

'How are we going to get back?'

'Now we know we can cross it,' the Mate said. The Kiwi kept silent.

TWO MORE THIRSTY HOURS OF stumbling through dense brush and a strange road opened up in front of us. It was a pipeline, as big around as a rubbish can, creating straight lines through the damp tangle of green. It seemed to be going around the mountain rather than up, but we walked on top of it for a while, striding free again at last. The pipeline led to the first flat piece of ground we'd seen since setting out, close to an opening in the canopy with a spectacular view of Rainmaker. We'd missed it by miles. The Mate was too tired to swear.

At least we'd found a place to camp. I'd been picturing having to tie ourselves to the trees to keep from rolling down those steep slopes or sleeping jammed into tree roots with ants crawling over us all night. Instead we gathered leaves and wood for a fire and explored. There were coconut palms just uphill, and a real road, not far behind the pipeline, which led down to a tidy plantation, still in use, full of some kind of bright red flower spikes. Knowing we weren't supposed to be there, we backtracked, but not before seeing that the odd road seemed to end with the plantation and was not a likely route for descending the mountain next day.

The Kiwi climbed a coconut palm to get milk as a mixer for the Mate's much-discussed rum toddies. In the crown of the tree, the ants found him, and he threw the coconuts down fast and slid down faster. Coconut leaves and giant fern, piled high, made a springy bed, and there was plenty of dry brush for a fire. When camp was ready, we walked out along the giant pipeline to our view of Rainmaker and settled down, each with a coconut full of rum, to watch the giant fruit-bats fly into the sunset.

It would have all been worthwhile if someone had remembered to bring the insect repellent. We'd been sailing so long; we'd forgotten about biting bugs. A million flying horses with spears in their noses came out with the bats and, with remarkable single-mindedness, tried to reduce *Cachalot's* crew to bloodless dust. We fled back to the fire and our bed of leaves.

Hours later, I was still wide awake. It seemed pointless for everyone to be sleepless, so I sat with my back to the hillside and waved a banana frond over the other two. The Kiwi's head was on my ankle, which had gone all pins and needles. The Mate was sleeping with a deep, righteous peace. I sat waving my ridiculous leaf at the swarming insects until just before dawn, when suddenly the mosquitoes disappeared as if they'd never been, and the yelling cicadas turned off like a switch. I'd had a lot of time to think, sitting through the night. The Kiwi woke first, as if the sudden quiet disturbed him. The fire pit was still glowing in the warm darkness and the birds hadn't yet started their sleepy dawn chorus.

'Simon,' I said, continuing a conversation I'd been having with myself, 'do you think they just left, you know, John—the deckhand who was aboard before you—on that island in the Galápagos? How did they know he was really gone by choice? If we were late back, would the boat just sail on without us?'

'Would you care?' he yawned, and then he sat up and he kissed me.

THE MATE FOUND US LATER, dressed in banana leaves, mugging for the camera. Neither of us could quite look her in the eye, as if we'd gone and finished off the rum without her, but she didn't seem to notice or care. So we dressed her in banana leaves too and took a few more sleepy photos. Then it was time to head down the mountain.

I absolutely refused to cross the mudslide again. We followed the streambed: it was easier walking. We stumbled barefoot over invisible stones tumbled along the white stream's path. After several hours we came to a series of pools that were flat and calm and deep. Each was separated by a wall of rock serving as a dam. The river behind the last dam dropped straight down more than 300 meters. It looked as if the still water in the last pool lapped against sky. There was no way down on one side of the river. The Kiwi walked shakily out over the last dam, and it looked as if he were walking a tightrope across the sky. He stumbled once.

'Don't leave us, Simon!' the Mate called plaintively. When Simon waved from the far side, the Mate and I quickly found a safer route, choosing to cross over one of the inland dams.

The sheer track beside the waterfall looked as if it had been made by goats. There were no handholds, not a single bit of greenery to cling to, just crumbling yellow clay and rock. It was as bad as the mudslide, and more exposed. The Mate scrambled down first, mostly on her rump, sometimes sliding on loose gravel as it came away. The Kiwi went behind her, but more slowly, occasionally stopping to help me with my pack, which I'd unslung and was inching down in front of me. We skidded ourselves and our gear down, bit by bit. I was almost weeping with fright by the time we finally put our feet on flat ground at the bottom of the falls. The town and the road were just ahead. We could hear dogs barking and smell cooking fires.

'Were you scared, Nat?' I asked then, feeling a deep shame now that the overwhelming height fear was gone.

'Oh, no,' the Mate said. 'Not at all.'

BY THE TIME WE'D TRUDGED back down to the village

126

I'd made up my mind not to go back to the boat.

'I want a shower tonight,' I said. 'And a hotel bed.'

The Mate shrugged. She'd made it clear she just wanted a meal that mooed.

We got it all from Sally, who'd been sleeping on the couch in the marina lobby when we arrived, long brown legs arranged artfully across the cushions. She made it clear that we were grossly dirty foreigners and needed to shower before dinner. She didn't particularly approve of our sharing a room, either. The Kiwi ducked his head and said he would just go back to the boat since he didn't have money for a separate room anyway, but Nat and I shouted him down, then offered him the floor.

Sally walked us to our room, mini-dress swishing, bare feet dancer-graceful, long black hair flipping from side to side, somehow managing to convey that whatever the grubby masses got up to was really beneath her notice.

The room turned out to have a huge double bed and very little floor space. We relented and offered to share the bed, but the Kiwi chose the floor. Even after the fitful night on the mountain and a solidly carnivorous meal, I found it difficult to settle into sleep. Here we all were, even on land crammed into a small space again with no hope for privacy. And for a small person—I discovered—the Mate could snore like a rhino.

WHEN WE GOT BACK TO the boat in the morning there were Things To Do before setting sail for Tonga. CW pointedly refrained from asking about our adventure and I found myself emphasizing the difficulties whenever the subject did come up.

Since I was on kid-watch all day, I decided to take the children and go boat-hopping—visit some of the other yachts. All the other boats in harbor seemed to keep in touch with one another over radio and even sail together, or at least meet regularly at each island stop, often delivering goods and groceries to friends on the various islands. There was a sense of community I'd never suspected among these yachties. They weren't wealthy people, for the most part, but couples or families who'd sold their houses and often built their own boats to give their children a chance to see the world. One boat named the *Odyssey* looked like a barn inside, with huge wooden beams, its thick hull formed from cement. The owners had left their jobs behind to find a new way of living, staying in port for months at a time, working and schooling their kids before moving on, often sailing to the next island with others from their floating community. There were exceptions. A few tough souls traveled alone.

A man near the docks was working on a beached catamaran he'd sailed by himself around the world, its dual cabins narrow and claustrophobic. He was eager to lend both tools and stories and gave Simon a wire brush to get the rust off the propane tanks used for *Cachalot's* stove. He told Simon that the largish patch he was fitting onto one hull was to mend a hole punched by a sperm whale that stove him in with no provocation, and who then compounded the insult by peering in through the hole at him.

Our Captain was skeptical.

'Sperm whales don't ram boats,' he said. 'Boats likely ram sleeping whales, since whales don't echo-locate when they log at the surface. It's also possible the boats are really ramming containers that have fallen off barges and are floating subsurface.'

'I know what I saw,' said the catamaran owner. 'And it was a giant eye looking in at me, gloating. Can't believe you follow those devils at night.' And his tone implied that he truly didn't believe it.

Most of the yachties didn't seem to know what to do with the researchers. Sperm whales were known to be dangerous and best avoided. And why sail so far and stay on an island for only four days? Bringing the kids along they clearly understood. I found being a nanny here had a certain cachet.

One of the teenage daughters off the cement-hulled *Odyssey* was on the docks chatting to Simon while he wire-brushed rust off our fuel tanks. He was obviously enjoying himself. I stomped past them with the kids, letting it be known that we were off to watch a film on board the yacht out of Hawaii. Nathalie just finished shopping for canned goods and joined us, joking rather too loudly that she wanted to meet the good-looking Hawaiian mate with the tribal tattoo around his ankle. The Hawaiian boat turned out to be unbearably luxurious below decks, with fine woodwork and upholstery, freshwater showers, a water-maker, fridge, dishwasher and VCR. The children stared at the film without moving for an hour while the rest of us talked.

Nathalie kept saying it was time to jump ship. But to me the Hawaiian couple had oddly unfocused goals and an ennui that accepted the luxuries with no obvious pleasure, although they were quite willing to share their space. They hinted that they, as well as a number of the other yachts, would be willing to take us aboard if we felt *Cachalot* was too uncomfortable or unconventional. It was as if the community had already discussed it.

It seemed as if *Cachalot's* mission had invested me with some purpose after all. Even after all the homesickness and discomfort, I just couldn't imagine sailing this road without the research being a part of it. Being a nanny or even crew on another yacht, however luxurious, seemed utterly pointless. What would be the reason for being out here if we weren't chasing whales?

SIMON HAD CHATTED WITH THE girl off *Odyssey* with a good deal of pleasure. He wrote later in his journal that it was a relief not to be bound up in all the tension and complaints aboard *Cachalot* for a while and just to have a wee natter about nothing.

It was hard for him not knowing if he'd be able to get funding to continue with the expedition, once they hit New Zealand. His recent letters from home weren't reassuring either. His mother had moved out; his father was already dating; the whole family sounded as if it was falling apart. He just wanted to keep moving. The Yank Nanny (and what did she want from him anyway?) had brought up the missing

130

crewman, John, and Simon had ignored her questions for other diversions. But what had really happened? The ship couldn't have abandoned him, could it? Simon hardly felt comfortable asking that question. But it had hung over his head every landfall, keeping him close, as if the policies of the boat didn't already discourage lingering on land. Would it be so bad to be left behind? Samoa had so much boat traffic, he was pretty sure he could find a berth, on the *Odyssey* maybe—she was heading home to Whangarei, New Zealand. But he doubted he'd ever jump ship. He couldn't just desert *Cachalot.*

The *Odyssey's* daughter left after inviting the crew over for drinks, just as Simon was getting around to wondering where Nat and the Yank had got to. He decided he'd better check the inside of the tank he was wire-brushing on the docks, maybe take a look with a flashlight, make sure there were no pinholes. The cap was stuck—he hoped that didn't mean the rust had gone through—but he gave it a good rap and finally it twisted off.

He looked inside. The mouth of the bottle was half blocked by a wad of folded, waterproof paper. It was a note from the missing crewman.

AFTER OUR CREW'S VISIT ABOARD the *Odyssey*, we headed back to *Cachalot,* the current with us. All of us were rosy after a beer or two. Simon stopped rowing the dinghy.

'There's something I want to show you two.'

'Here? Now? In front of all these people?'

'Don't be a dag. Here, read this. I found it in one of the propane tanks this arvo.' He unfolded the letter and read out loud:

I'm hiding this note where you will find it too late to stop me. I wish I could tell you I am leaving, but I don't want to start a fight, so I'll just go. I hope you can understand. I got a letter when we arrived at the Darwin Station, and I couldn't tell anyone because I thought you'd think badly of me. My girl back home wrote that she is going to have a baby. I have to go home and talk her out of it. Or not, I just don't know anything right now except I'm miserable and I have to go. I have to go right now. I'm sorry, but it's a relief to finally be doing something.

'That's very bad, eh? Why the stupid boy put it in the tank?'

I imagined for a brief moment what the captain might feel on land. At sea he had a stable crew that worked together because it had to. Land introduced diversity, instability, options, temptations, chaos. It allowed us to be influenced by home.

'Nathalie,' I asked, 'how did you know for sure you all hadn't just left John stranded on a beach somewhere when you kept sailing?'

The Mate squeaked. 'I am sure I tell you,' she said. 'The captain go to the airport and check the passenger list. John's name is on this list.'

All that worry for nothing. 'Bags not me,' Simon said.

WHEN WE GOT BACK TO *Cachalot*, the handsome Hawaiian couple were waiting for us on the dock, waving a newspaper folded back to a picture of our hostess, Sally. She looked far more tarted up than usual; smooth skin overlaid with heavy make-up and eyeshadow. There was also a picture of her new pilot boyfriend, his familiar face shown grinning from every chin. The article said the pilot was flying Sally to New Zealand for her long-awaited operation, and that she planned to stay on and dance in a nightclub that he also owned. Her ageing parents were coming with her. Auckland's Polynesian community reckoned they were gaining a celebrity.

'I knew she was fa'afafine,' the Hawaiian mate said, hugging his partner happily. 'You owe me twenty dollars, bro.'

'What is this?' Nathalie said in some confusion, so the Hawaiians hugged her too, making her giggle.

WE SET SAIL THAT EVENING for Tonga, knowing other humans would be making the same passage, looking for us along the way, aware of our absence if we didn't arrive, on radio if we chose to speak. The immense horizon felt less empty. Family and crew shared the evening meal above decks at sunset and watched the hulking wrecks at the mouth of Samoa's harbor become oscillating flecks on the waves.

Bad Morning

It is impossible to meet a whale-ship on the
ocean without being struck by her near
appearance. The vessel under short sail, with
look-outs at the mast-heads, eagerly scanning
the wide expanse around them, has a totally
different air from those engaged in a regular
voyage.

—'Currents and Whaling,' *Moby-Dick*

I WOKE TO FOUR SMALL eyes peering hopefully and
shut my own lids tightly in exasperation. What a way to wake
up, I crabbed silently and refused to open my eyes again,
seeing behind closed lids the baby's crooked smile as the
cold, sticky little fingers pinched my sleep-warmed arm and
then scrabbled at my nose.

The older boy would have that haunted, hunted look
in his eyes. I wasn't on kid-watch yet. Why should I have to
respond at all? I'd ignore him, that's what I'd do, and I
flicked the covers over my face and groaned just as someone
snatched up the baby.

I could feel the boy hovering, irritatingly. He
hummed a little under his breath and I felt the air of him
swish past. He must have been rocking back and forth from
the mast, where it grew below decks like a metal tree trunk.
I was smothering under my thin blanket. The baby was
screaming now in the galley, not a meters away. I knew if I
could just smile and catch her up on the bunk there'd be no

134

screaming—for a while. But I burrowed deeper under the blanket and sweated. It wasn't my *turn* yet. The boy was so close, I could see the red sheen of him through the cloth. I gasped under the cover and turned it back angrily. There was no one there.

I breathed a great sigh of cool air and a little towhead popped around the chart table, blue eyes heavily circled in scarlet, puffy skin, no smile at all until I chose to—or not. I watched him narrowly as he watched me, our eyes locked as he slowly began to rock on the mast again, back and forth, head swiveling.

The baby screamed. If there were someone here to make me smile, I could smile at him, I thought, but an anger welled up in me and I swung up and out, stomping to the head, only a few paces away, the boy following centimeters behind until I shut the door in his face, sighed again, and locked the door. I saw the latch lift gently and almost screamed in frustration.

Leave me alone, I thought raggedly, and pumped energetically at the toilet siphon, flushing away his morning stink. It was 5:30 a.m. I had half an hour to get some breakfast into me before I was on. I felt nauseated. I'll have three hours to myself at noon, I told myself firmly. All I have to do is smile.

I came out of the head and, with the roll of a wave, stretched my lips over my teeth without saying a word. He threw himself at me, his hard head catching me in the sternum, a small bare foot stepping heavily onto my instep. I squeezed him gingerly, catching his bony bird shoulders and holding him a little away. He leaned his head back to smile up at me, his hands stroking my arms while my skin shivered away like a horse shaking off a fly.

I WAS ON WATCH LATER when the captain came up and changed course. I held the boy out of the way while the Kiwi helped put a reef in the mainsail. The captain started to ask me to take in the preventer, then muttered a 'never mind' and came back and did it himself. I know how the boy feels, I cursed silently, when no one lets him do anything. It makes one feel small and angry. And I hugged the child fiercely this time. But his eyes were on his father, his face unreadable. What will he remember?

136

7.
Kingdom of Tonga:
November–December

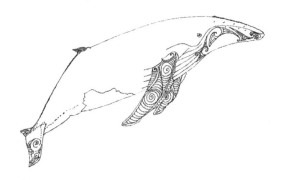

Whale Food

And the breath of the whale is frequently
attended with such an insupportable smell, as
to bring on a disorder of the brain.
    —'Uloa's South America', *Moby-Dick*

THERE ARE BLACK AND WHITE whales before the
mouth of the wide, green channels of Va'vau. They are like
the whales from home. Humpback whales. They are bubble
feeding. Globes of green light roll up towards the sunlight
from the dark water. A chain of glowing color rises while the
seabirds scream and dive, bare moments of tiny frantic fish
massing at the surface, webbed in by the circle of lights—of
bubbles. Sudden dark whale bodies rise from the ocean like
gigantic, black-pointed mussel shells, filling and stretching
soft, pale undersides with many hundreds of liters of water
and eels and fish and, once, a startled gannet. Gulping throat
pouches swell white and pink with effort. Greedy mussel
mouths clap shut, giant tongues push forward and the water
squirts past wriggling invertebrates stranded between hairy
mouth plates, layer upon layer straining and tangling small
life-forms while the water rushes back into the ocean.

Then there is only mouth, big as an automobile,
licking down tiny ocean species into a throat no larger than
a grapefruit. The gannet escapes, bedraggled, when the jaws
part and gulp again. There is still a concentration of fishes
roiling the water as the last of the green bubbles rise and
burst back into air.

The humpback whales wallow at the surface for a while. Accordion-pleated underthroats, still pink with warm blood, slowly collapse back into sleek whale shape as the water runs out and the fish slide down into warm, dark, internal cupboards. The whales roll and jostle, long white pectoral fins waving in the air and slapping the water with sharp cracks of sound. They blow several warm, stinking breaths and dive again.

We have to leave the humpbacks finally, to follow a small pod of sperm whales passing farther offshore, heading away from the seductive green of the wooded islands, swimming northwest towards a distant, smoking volcano that seems to rise out of the water like a pyramid. No one has ever been able to watch sperm whales feed, miles deep in their ocean trenches. There are stories of them battling squid larger than our boat, puckered scars on their skin from giant squid beaks. An oil drum was found in a butchered sperm whale. There are the enduring stories of a man living in the belly of the whale, another of a man losing his leg to the great white whale. But it seems clear that far more whales have been eaten by humans and ground for cosmetics and pet food than ever entered our mythologies by deigning to swallow the Jonahs and the Ahabs and Bartleys of our world.

On 25th August 1891, James Bartley, a thirty-five-year-old sailor on the Star of the East, was swallowed by a sperm whale off the Falkland Islands.

—Julian Barnes
A History of the World In 10 Chapters

Up the Mast

To fifty chosen sylphs, of special note,
We trust the important charge, the petticoat.
Oft we have known that sevenfold fence to fail,
Though stiff with hoops and armed with ribs of
whale.

—Alexander Pope, *The Rape of the Lock*

WORDS ON A PAGE AND the smoking cone of the
volcano drew the sperm whales like a smaller sun as we
turned away from the kingdom of Tonga and headed
seaward again.

The triangular mountain jutted up from a glassy
ocean; clouds swirled about its peak like flags waving in a sky
of blue foil. It was more magnificent than Adam's most
horrible imaginary monster, made more terrible because
fading behind us was the softer beauty of unreachable
coconut-wooded islands with deep channels and the
unmistakable signs of other people inhabiting their shores.

We were all, except the captain, leaning out over the
railing of the boat, staring longingly back towards the
Tongan islands, while listening to the distinctive, toothy
clicking of sperm whales.

The captain, helmsman of his own tiny kingdom, kept
his eyes on the beckoning volcano and towards the open sea
and the voices of the sea creatures. Adam, the ship's
emotional barometer, started to wail hopelessly, 'Stop
studying whales, Dada! Go study islands!'

It must have been a magic phrase. Or it might have been the mundane lentils we ate every night, or an entropy spell cast by CW, or the fact that the Mate had brushed her teeth in the last of our good drinking water, but the Captain turned his preoccupied gaze away from the siren call of the sea, and he turned *Cachalot* back towards the peaceful land. He did not, however, let us set foot ashore for the time being, as his calendar—even given all the time changes—indicated that we were landing on a Sunday again.

And so, once upon a time, on a tiny boat in a warm and tropical harbor, there was a party going on in the open cockpit. The evening lentils had been cooked with the last can of tomato sauce and the last clove of garlic. The Mate shared around a previously unsuspected bottle of rum, which she poured liberally into the no-longer-quite-so-endless mugs of tea made from the very last dribs and drabs of fresh water in the tanks. The captain had brought out his last bar of carefully hoarded chocolate. Adam was given a new cardboard and foil sword, and the baby wore a helmet, fashioned by Simon from a new rubber potty plunger, which buoyantly repelled all sword swipes, accidental or otherwise. It was a merry crew that settled into the evening with hopes for new visions (and supplies) coming with the new day.

'Adam wants to go camping,' I announced after we'd eaten. Adam beamed.

'Why don't I make him a tent under the galley table, and you two . . .' I leered cheerfully at the Captain and CW, '. . . can have a little privacy in the aft cabin for once.'

The captain volunteered to make the tent and, knocking back his rum tea, planted a hearty kiss on CW's surprised face. After rapidly assembling Adam's camp, he climbed below decks before anyone could change the plan (though CW did insist he take the baby, whom she stuffed in through a porthole). Seeing that CW was planting her backside firmly above boards, the Mate exited the party for her forward cabin with an unladylike snort of disgust.

CW picked up the Mate's drink and swilled it. When she'd stopped coughing, she wiped her eyes and poured more rum into her own and then the crew's tea mugs.

Simon and I glanced at each other, and his hands grasped my toes in the shadows. CW, if she saw, let the activity float into the restricted region of the unobservable, the black spot of her mind, a common phenomenon among the denizens of our crowded little kingdom on the sea.

'Am I a terrible person?' CW asked her audience, not for the first time. 'Do I deserve to be treated like a leper?' I knew from experience she was referring to the Mate.

'I wish you would talk to her,' I said. 'She's really not so bad . . .'

'Oh, I've tried,' CW said bitterly. 'There's nothing more I can do. On the yacht we visited in Samoa, the captain's wife said she couldn't believe what I had to put up with. She said she wouldn't put up with it!' CW seemed to hold her breath a little, looking at us sideways as if to see how we would take this radical idea of her setting limits.

I looked anxiously at Simon.

'Well,' he said tentatively, 'what else is there to do?'

144

CW seemed to collapse a little in on herself, her shoulders hunched and her hands hanging limply.

'Have I done something wrong?' she wailed while we patted her and stroked her arms. No, no, we said, you are a good person, we like you, everything will be okay. And Simon and I looked at each other and longed for landfall.

Hours later, we were all aglow with camaraderie and rum, though at past two in the morning CW still seemed unwilling to join the captain in the aft cabin. Opportunity was fading with the night stars, and I was getting a little fed up with foot-fondling.

I watched Simon sip his tea with a feeling of something important slipping away. We'd barely had a chance to talk since Samoa. I jumped up.

'Well, it's getting late. I may just go up on the bow and do a bit of starwatching before turning in.'

'Really?' slurred CW. 'Is it nice up there?'

'Or I may just go to bed now,' I said pointedly. 'Are you turning in?'

'Oh, yes, I guess it's about that time,' she said, settling against her floaty cushion with that just-one-last-drink look.

I watched in surprise as Simon took the mug out of her hand.

'Here, I'll take care of that for you,' he said. 'Shall I bring up everyone's toothbrushes?'

'Simon, you are so sweet,' CW said emotionally. 'You are just such a good person. Isn't he just the perfect man?' She winked at me.

'Umph,' I grunted noncommittally, swaying a bit where I stood.

The night was so quiet, the ship barely creaked. There was an early-morning anticipation in the air, although it was still velvet-dark and warm. A rainbow halo surrounded each brilliant star. Rum tea, I thought, or a storm coming.

Miracle of miracles, CW went to bed after brushing her teeth in the bucket of seawater I pulled up, leaning over so far with the heavy bucket I almost tipped myself over the rail. Here, falling into the harbor might be a laugh, but I shivered thinking what it would mean out on the open sea. Our ship was so small, encompassed on all sides by that deep and living serpent of water girdling the world. The new land just beyond the railing looked like any tangled Eden. The sky felt lower here. I imagined reaching up and laying my palms on the shadowed clouds. Clearly the ship was really clinging sideways to the thin middle of the world, the planet barely turning beneath its hull. Even the moon hung oddly angled in the sky. It was an amazing feeling, like being up in the highest tier of a tall building, squashed up against the ceiling of the sky while my feet, far below, were being sprayed by salty splashes of moonlight.

Simon climbed back up through the hatch and stood beside me. Only the hairs on our arms touched, sending goosebumps along my flesh. The effect was equal to that of a full-frontal assault to someone whose physical world had been made up of seasickness, barked shins, and being alternately hugged and pummeled by children for months. I gasped for breath. I could see Simon looking at me in the

146

dim moonlight. It made me feel solid, despite the cushiony, absorbing night. No more taking care of people, watching children, bolstering egos, worrying about hurt feelings. Away from the daylight and the heat and the work, in the darkness, I felt real.

I took Simon's hand and he held mine hard.

'Come on!' I whispered and tiptoed up to the forward decks. The light was on in the captain's cabin. We crept by the lighted hatch, and I headed for the highest ground we could reach.

'Wait!' Simon hissed; he'd paused near the half-open hatch.

'No, no!' I heard, the faraway cry of an albatross. 'No, no!'

Simon stumbled over and put his arms around me.

'That's an ill-luck sound for some poor sod tonight.'

I imagined the baby's hard little heels kicking the researchers in their bunk bed and started to laugh, gasping and almost crying. I pulled away from Simon and yanked myself up the first handhold on the mast, climbing as fast as I could, as high, as far away . . .

'Wait, ya silly Yank, you'll fall!' Simon hesitated a moment and then followed, the wires clanging and clattering in the quiet night. He clambered into the crow's nest and managed to wedge himself in, hearing me laugh and not seeing my tears in the dark.

'Look at the stars!' I said and climbed over the protective rail onto the thin crosstie.

He reached for me then and held me safe, him

standing in the crow's nest and me unprotected on the crosstie. He held me tightly and it felt good and I felt good and I was so close to the thick night air and the stars. And who would notice, far below, if, after a while, one small kingdom far away by the sea rocked gently to a rhythm not altogether of the waves?

And does writing it down make it so?

'YOU KNOW,' THE MATE CONFIDED privately, once ashore on Tonga, 'it is true that standards change at sea, usually to get worse, in fact. Myself, I do not like the skinny little boys. I prefer a man to have a man's shape.'

'You mean broad at the top with a narrow butt?'

'Yes. That is it exactly.'

'I've met parsnips that have that configuration,' I said. 'And glass men.'

The Nanny's Tale

(Wherein the Nanny tells all to two friends while surrounded by marauding pigs)

THERE WAS A RUMBLE IN the darkness: a herd of Tongan piggies heading towards us. The Kiwi, the Mate and I leapt up as a dozen black and red swine of varying sizes thundered out of the dark, bumping and veering past. Pigs were the theme of Tonga. They were everywhere, trotting past on the road, sleeping in shadows, hanging out on corners, watching passers-by with bored eyes. They scuttled past in family groups in search of unoccupied gardens or rubbish piles, both of equal appeal.

My crewmates had asked for a particular story, the one of my circumstances before the boat. I'd heard theirs, in the bits and pieces one gets between waves, and they'd heard most of my tales—except for this one. It was the end of a long day exploring a new land. The Kiwi and the Mate were silent as we found a small hillock and sat down, in the dark yard that surrounded two round, leaf-roofed tourist bungalows we'd rented—an oddly flat luxury for one brief night on Tonga. The piggies rumbled around us in the yard like a toy train off its track.

I waited for someone to ask again. I must have mentioned what I did for work in winter, when I was inland, or they'd have not asked. But I'd come to appreciate being 'just the Nanny' aboard ship, after realizing how the yachties had viewed me back in Samoa. Not a Scientist. Not a

Naturalist. Not even an Artisan's First Assistant, which was the story I was holding on to now. It made sense to the yachties that a young woman would sail around the world as a Nanny. It fitted in with what those boatmen and women expected, and they made me welcome aboard their ships. It was the researchers the yachties didn't understand, felt uncomfortable talking to, couldn't place. It seemed important to belong.

'Living on land is like being a beached whale,' I wish I'd said, 'always at the mercy of someone else's agenda. Or perhaps it's only the opposite of being at sea. So many demands, expectations, bills, taxes to remember to pay. So many people. Sometimes I felt like a nuclear reactor melting down, ready to burn a hole to the center of the earth. Out here the elements, wind and rain, rule our lives completely, pushing us forward or holding us back, surging. There, human-made power always seemed about to go wildly out of control. Making us edgy, arrhythmic. Unkind.'

The Glass Bitch in an Atomic Age

The Universe is made of stories, not of atoms.
—Muriel Rukeyser (1913–80)

HER LIFE WILL BE GLASS in winter, water in summer. The blowpipe twirls in the glory hole, the glassman dips into the glowing crucible, jacks a neck into the gather. Her lips blow gently on one end of the rotating pipe while he sits, hands in constant motion, concentrating on speed, on heat, on the expanding bubble of air growing like a golden seed in the superheated orb of molten glass.

The glassblower's talk is centered on two images: the spinning globe on the pipe, and the small crescents of his new assistant's breasts, glimpsed when she leans over to shield his hands from the heat with a wooden paddle. He tells her he'd like to paddle her; claims she'd be blushing if the heat of the furnaces didn't already have her half boiled. He seems to want to embarrass her, make her mess up, drop the pipe, stick the pliant taffy bubble to the cement floor. He hands off the pipe to her, almost throwing it, with a fling that kicks the even bubble out of true when she catches it badly. Her hands are not as quick as his.

He is the master craftsman. He tells her this—best on the east coast, top ten west coast, he says, while sweat or tears run down her chin for the bent bubble of glass that must be thrown away into the cullet bucket. Only way to learn is to screw up, he says kindly. Glass is not worth crying over until it is out of the annealer, not a finished piece until the agitated molecules are slowed and cooled. Glass is a supercooled liquid, never stops moving over the years. Eventually it will sag and slump and thicken at the bottom like her young body, moving now like a dancer over the cement floor of the shop.

The spin of gravity will suck them all down to the earth's molten core in the end. He tells her that he believes this the way he trusts his skill for turning glass. Never stop moving, he says. Never let the glass stop spinning. Never cry over broken glass, and never touch glass with unprotected hands. He watches her breasts swinging as she stoops to touch, half visible through the cotton shirt that is already sticking to her in the heat. He groans dramatically and crashes the pipes out of the cooling bucket, slides them into the warming garage so that chunks of unannealed glass pop off the pipes from the sudden change in temperature and fly across the room.

He shouts at her to put her glasses on: *Godsballs*, does she want to lose an eye? He slams a pipe into her hands, brawny arms caging her from behind, maneuvering her hesitating feet forward with the pressure of his hips. He crowds her up to the furnaces, slides open the door and guides the pipe with their four hands down into the pool of molten glass in a desiccating blast of heat. She gasps and turns her head from the stink of burning hair, but he tightens his grip, his own arm hair a fine fur of asbestos. His eyes are on the spinning pipe in the pool, his callused paws slide down to cup her reddening fingers. Deeper, he rasps, lips to her ear, start at a steep angle and slide back. The girl shrinks

152

from the heat, backing up against him where he stands, a muscled wall against the destroying heat.

He slides shut the gates of hell, leaving the relative coolness of sopping shirts and scorched air. The girl lets go the pipe and won't take it back, ducking away. He laughs and lets her splash her arms and neck in the water bucket. It flecks her red skin with leaf fragments of blackened newsprint, fallout from an atomic blast. His own thick forearms are not even flushed.

She asks him about the scars across his arms while he starts to shape the bubble. He gives her a pontil rod—a punty. She can spin its smaller circumference more easily in her less agile hands. He comments on the way she seems to glide across the floor: two steps to the honeypot, the crucible; turn and step to the metal marvering table; an awkward swipe of the arms to shape the glass bullet-tipped; a quick backward spin—the feet are pure grace—and she is in position at his side. It's a terrible punty, the glass tip too hot and shapeless. She holds herself tense, ready for him to transfer the bubble from blowpipe to punty. He ignores her, sits on his bench, turning the pipe, letting things cool down. He finally waves her away. Keep practicing; that was about as useful as a chihuahua with a two-ton dick, he says. Next time, pick up a chunk of color on that punty—the shape's not good but it will work for color. She's frustrated and he grins. You move like a dancer, he says again, that's why I hired you. This whole process is a dance. And she blushes.

Shape that color into a Hershey's Kiss, he says, and stands the mouthpiece of the blowpipe on his booted foot, holding the bubble upright with a pair of diamond shears. For a moment the turning stops. His sudden lack of motion makes her breathless. Bring it, he starts, just as she spins away from the metal table with a perfect broad-bottomed triangle of color drooping from the punty rod. Too cold! he snaps, and they both dive for the glory hole to reheat. Then he's back at the bench, and now the girl has things too hot. Pull a finger out and use it, he growls, you have to watch the way the color moves. Finally she spins across the floor to where he stands, steps into position and drops the triangular Kiss of yellow onto the cooling bubble.

He snips the taffy-like triangle away from the punty. The shears take a moment to smooth the medallion of color down over the bubble, and then he is back at the glory hole. She puts the punty in the cullet bucket and comes to stand beside him, unsure what to do next.

He seems calmer now. He turns the pipe in the glory hole with one hand and reaches over with the other to grab the neckline of her shirt. She's standing just far enough away that he can't quite look down at her small breasts. He pretends he can. Sod off, she says. But she doesn't move away, and his eyes brighten.

Door, he says, his voice so husky from hours of glass fumes, it matches the tone of the furnace exactly. Door! he says again, and she jumps to close the door around the end of the pipe. He hands the pipe off and stands beside her for a moment to be sure she turns it evenly. Keep it moving, he says, and don't bend over.

He makes a perfect glass bullet on the tip of a new pontil rod and swaps with her, takes over the bigger blowpipe and sits at the bench. She heats the punty too deep in the furnace again and brings it over, the tip a shapeless glowing lump. What is this, Chernobyl? he shouts, and slams his jacks down on the square of beeswax he uses for lubricating his tools. The sweet smoke of burning honey fills the air. Cool it on the marvering table, he snaps. Flash it once in the furnace and bring it back. *Now.*

She scrambles, hands fumbling, but her feet bringing her precisely into position. He scrapes excess wax off the delicate, soft-metal tongs that are his jacks, his other fingers, and he takes hold of the heated end of the punty, using the jacks to guide it to the base of the glass bubble in a cloud of hot bee-scent. The punty sticks to the bubble, dead centre, and then slides a fraction. Relax your hands, he growls, turn with me. He makes a score line across the top of the bubble, and smacks the pipe, ringing metal on metal. The bubble cracks away from the pipe along the score, which is now the mouth of a vessel, but the weight, suddenly transferring to the punty, makes the girl stagger.

He swears and the girl tenses up again as he takes the punty from her.
Not *too bad*, he says, but never let the bubble drop like that. I can probably get it back on centre, but it wastes time, and it won't be the same. Bring the paddle and shield my hands. Get in my way and I will paddle you.

At the bench he inserts the fingers of his jacks into

the molten interior of the bubble, opening it up like a flower as it spins against his careful pulling pressure. It is the loveliest moment of every piece. His eyes gleam with a reflection of glass. He plays with the shape, pulling and pressing, elongating with jacks and paddles. He uses a heavy wad of soaked newspaper to pad his hand, the weight of the vessel opening into his palm while it scorches the top layers of wet paper to dust, as close as he can get to hot glass without melting his flesh. I am the master, he says. When the smooth glide of fingers over honey changes to the rattle of metal on cooling glass, he hands the final shape, a fluted vase, into the annealer and cracks the punty away, leaving a small umbilical scar. He is quiet, takes a moment to drink some water and looks at the expectant face of his assistant, awaiting his praise or curses. But she is looking at the scars again, on the forearm he raises to wipe his mouth.

My master's name was Furio Cecchi, he says. Furious Furio. Finest glass artisan outside Italy. He'd blown glass with his stepfather since he was eleven, on the island of Murano, near Venice. Had to take paternity leave away from the heat of the furnaces to father his own children, but none of his offspring could ever blow glass. Glassblowers tend to have girl children, if any, and females weren't allowed near the furnaces. He could make a matched set of Ratachelli goblets, each graduated down an exact millimeter in height, in less than twenty minutes each. The man was a machine.

The glassman holds up both forearms, hands clenched, exposing a white crosshatching of scars. I was his

156

best student. If I made a mistake, he'd lay hot jacks across my arm.

His face is a pale moon. You won't ever get burned working with me, Red, he says. Not by accident, not ever. If you stay with me, if you can hack it, you'll learn glass. Come, I'll start the next bubble. Stand beside me and watch the angle of the gather.

SHE FALLS ASLEEP THAT NIGHT on a hard futon, imagining the glassman dreaming her; too tired to do more than picture the sweaty clefts where cloth hugged the dark creases of her armpits, a roundness of breast and buttocks, fractured body parts. A seed of air swells in a hot bubble. There is molten glass running through his veins. The crucible is glowing, and everything is spinning.

THE DARK HUMPED SHAPES OF piggies rootled nearby. I felt unfocused from my internal meandering, unsure how much I'd said, and how much viewed privately within my own memory/imagination. My crewmates sat silently, stunned mullets under the barrage of strange, uncomfortable words. Our land lives had become utterly irrelevant at last.

'Good-oh,' the Kiwi finally said, patting my shoulder awkwardly.

'Yes. It was very interesting,' the Mate said, in her clipped way, and started to laugh.

'Ten years,' I said. 'Ten years of that.'

And then it was morning, and time to go to sea.

157

NO WHALES. NONE. NADA, NIENTE. We are flying 'at a rate of knots' towards New Zealand. This whole passage may take only a couple of weeks or even less. We have already passed the Kermadec Islands—couldn't stop, no anchorage, the captain said. Missed Minerva Reef as well. Once upon a time, the old whaling journals say, there were so many whales in these South Pacific waters that every few nautical miles they would find one dead of natural causes. Dead in the water.

8.
The Whale Road

Writing Home

I have bedimmed
The noontide sun, called forth the mutinous winds,
And 'twixt the green sea and the azured vault,
Set roaring war—to the dread rattling thunder . . .
But this rough magic,
I here abjure . . .
    — Shakespeare, *The Tempest*, Act V, Scene 1

WAVES ROLL THEIR MOUNTAINOUS BELLIES past rows of porthole eyes. Bunks try to shake us out like salt. No human sounds, just lentils rattling their bones in nested bottles. The hull cries, and water sighs and groans from wind slap. Every living soul is webbed in, quiet-scared. The captain is up on deck, too long and too quiet. No knowing if a wave took him in the dawn hours. Pull the sheet overhead and put off looking. It's easier to hide. He must be tired.

Last midnight the big wind blew up. The sail's lifeline parted and threw wet canvas to the deck. Our Mate blames the captain for not liking land, for hurrying us away from our last port of call. For not knowing the halyard was frayed. He's the scapegoat now, up in the storm. Some other boat will find us. Maybe. A low blue hull in steely grey, matching the juddering waves in such a violent, empty place. I wonder if anyone will ever read this, back home—wherever that is now. Can you imagine?

It is important to lift up, sometimes, look out an eyelet to the world while vision spins. It feels like a morning after hard drinking. The portholes open to an alien planet. Our ship bucks and shivers on the skin of an uneasy beast, its hide ripples. This is no time to be ill, don't think it, but quickly drop down again to jam in against the pitch, shoulders digging in one side, heels the other. Cover the face and go somewhere else.

SUNLIGHT, NOW, STREAMING IN FROM up top. Squint into the light and see a single, ragged grey tennis-shoe, a pale red ankle bracing it across the cockpit. The captain's still with us. He's jammed in too: that tired shoe seems to reflect a grey face. Hard night.

The Mate is swearing, an angry mutter rumbling from the forward cabin. The boat is all harsh rattle and battered silence. It's easier to believe in the captain than be afraid. Something perversely exhilarating comes in on the storm air. There is a smell of wildness in it. Time to go up top soon.

My thoughts and handwriting fly up and down with the boat. Sadness for some home, left too far back. I haven't called in months. The captain never leaves the radio on. Doesn't like the things that bring land. The Mate whines about foul water and no meat. The captain shrugs: a water-maker could break, create more work for him. He won't take fish from this ocean, and everyone is hungry, tired of the rattling beans.

The dinghy trailing invisibly behind—maybe attached to its twisted rope—is a sorry inflatable, one wooden oar, one plastic oar, no motor, and the Mate says the harnesses are rotten. A box strapped on deck says Liferaft, but better to stay in the big boat in these seas, thanks. No rescuers galloping over this rolling plain.

The wind shrieks: no one jumps to answer. In all the rough activity nothing living moves. Is this fear? All rules and laws of the boat are suspended. No one rotates watch. No one scavenges in the galley or boils water for tea since a calmer yesterday. We are sand eels, heads buried down in a pebble substrate, tails waving free, while toothed things nibble our vulnerable ends. If the boat sank now, we would all—not the captain—dig down deeper and close milky eyes.

The captain knows Things To Do. His boat is hoven to, bobbing like a bitten apple in an angry ocean. The waves measure their height by twice our mast now. They roll in slowly, picking us up along smooth edges—an elevator running up the outside of bulging skyscrapers—then tip us down into troughs that scrape bottom on unfathomable trenches below.

The Kiwi says our Captain is a good sailor. The boy often sings that song. Better than fear. He heard that our Captain once, sailing solo on a different sea, and younger then, passed the test sent by an old hurricane. Other boats made safe harbor that day. Waves bigger than these were peaking in the middle, out to destroy. The captain sailed into the wind, smooth as a storm bird, until a giant picked up his boat, pitch-poled her, tumbling end over end, snapping her mast, bending her rudder. Somehow the Captain stayed aboard, clinging like seagull shit to that smashed hull. Somehow, the storm ripping into him, he made safe harbor.

That's why our Captain is a good sailor.

And yet, in moments of fear one wonders, does sailing a boat alone make him a good Captain of others? He's been on deck twenty hours now. His crew doesn't know how to help him help us. If he stops caring, if this wind continues, we can't count on him to save us.

Even in a storm it is possible to fall asleep, to wake into the clarity of afternoon light and a deep sky-blue. The captain sleeps in his bunk in the main cabin, arms flung across his face, toes nesting like naked mice in his shredded sneakers. No sign of the others. The pressure of a full bladder makes hiding less important, so get up, stagger to the head and back on the jointed funhouse plank that used to be a cabin floor. The locker below the ladder holds tangled orange harnesses—useless, the Mate said, so yank one out and trail it, half climbing, half falling, up the ladder and into the cockpit. The Kiwi is there, harnessed in, long bare feet braced across the pit, filthy in month-old singlet and shorts, long blond rattail dripping from the spray. The sunlight is a warm blanket across my shoulders. Feet braced opposite, carefully not touching, we stare into a shifting tower of impossible waves. Their murky grey sides are barely penetrated by the sun.

'How we gonna fix the sails?'

'Someone'll have to climb.'

If our shuddering boat is the fulcrum, the mast is a wildly waving splinter in the sky, about to dip into the wall of waves at the outside of each arc.

'Bags not me,' he says, putting thumb to forehead.

We sit in the sun, watching the mountains roll under. I feel good after those hard hours spent below. The air smells clear and bright. The sun is warm.

'It's lovely,' I say out loud.

'Oh, yeah.'

SO NOW I'M THINKING OF home again, and finally wondering if any of you know how long a minute can be—out here where time slows to stopping. I almost see the lives you live busy, blinkered, your sun racing to peer through one office window after the next, or glowering from inside the dark, lumpy forms of furnaces. Time we spend under this wider sky.

Who knew the world had such edges? So many days went by on land that were never noticed in their passing. Home is where we sat inside after dark, cold under artificial lights, rustling pages, blue ghosts flickering, ignoring each other.

No one could ignore the night sky out here, so full and bright it hurts sunburnt eyes. Most evenings, an hourglass sun pours into water through its own pinched waist on the horizon. The crew settles together on decks to eat their share of food and stare out over the waves. I search the endless horizon for the last bitter flash of light that winks green as the sun submerges, drowning us in watery dusk. Later, during watch, flocks of stars chase one another overhead in the upturned bowl of the sky. Time collapses while the universe turns. Orion flees the Scorpion towards morning.

Our storm began last night as an ugly clot on the horizon. I tried to steer around it, adjusting the tiller southish. Before an hour had passed, it was a black giant enveloping the yellow moon, Cronos eating his children. I reached down for a rain jacket, straightening up into Cronos' hot breath slamming into the boat. How fast it blew up! Our boat jumped in the sudden squall, skittered sideways. The boom snapped viciously, and I saw the captain's hands on the ladder—the good sailor in tune with his boat—just as the sails came down, hitting the decks with a massive wet bellow.

I never saw the captain tie down the wheel. I must have been watching the sky swallowing a struggling moon. Then the Captain was up on the deck hugging the mast as it rocked, yelling—steer to starboard!—the wheel immobile in my hands. The boom swung side to side, trying to throw him over as he clutched one-handed at a heavy sail shifting and flapping like a broken wing. I felt the rope choking the wheel, fumbled to loosen it, and the ship's wheel finally turned, angling her nose into the hot wind. The pressure around us subsided. Broken sails and the swinging boom relaxed for a moment, freeing the captain, who leapt back into the safety of the cockpit. In a few long moments we had lost our sails, almost lost the captain, and I never noticed, until he sent me below, that I was drenched and shaking, imagining the moon's chill screams.

I HAD FOUGHT TO BE allowed to take night watch, the only time any of us has truly alone, my time with the sky.

166

During the long, sweltering days I concentrate on the captain's children — shove the food in, wipe the shit off — and avoid the awful sun. We drink foul water, choke down the same dinner of lentils and rice, hear the Mate's numbing list of complaints and fault-finding. I try to calm the kids, listen to their mother's growing antipathy for the Mate and her own constant doubts. During the day I am ignored by the Kiwi; told by the captain, when I ask questions, that my place is with the children. Then I must face my own growing lethargy, constant nausea and fear. Why am I here? What will I do if I leave? Return home again, to more of the same?

On land I listened to others complain, fed their starving self-esteem, allowed anyone to tell me what my place was, my existence in their service. It was land-sickness sent me out here, running from hell to hell.

THE RHYTHM OF THE WAVES has changed. I want to tell you evening air is blowing up fine and fresh with a lightning smell of ozone. The storm has torn away more than our sails. Light is failing, and the wind is on the rise again. For the first time since becoming a fleck on this pitiless horizon, I am afraid. There is no moon. The billowing waves have eaten all my stars. The Kiwi shared the last beer with me, cold and shaken from where it rolled in the bilge. When it is finished, I will fold these pages very small. I am sending home the last of my love in an empty bottle, sealing it away from wind and water, giving it to the wicked ocean. We have become the waves now, cold and silent, floating free.

167

Finding Eden

He was wondrous to look upon, the whale rider. The
water streamed away from him and he opened his
mouth to gasp in the cold air. His eyes were shining
with splendor. His body dazzled with diamond spray.
Upon that beast he looked like a small tattooed figurine,
glistening and erect. He seemed, with all his strength,
to be pulling the whale into the sky . . .

—Witi Ihimaera, *The Whale Rider*

KAHUTIA TE RANGI, THE WHALE Rider, escaped from
his brother and became the whale, Paikea; rode the whale
from Hawaiki, the mythical island of the ancestors, to
Aotearoa, Land of the Long White Cloud. Kahutia Te Rangi,
who became Paikea, lived to have many children and
populated Aotearoa with his offspring. He settled finally in
Whangara. Whangara, because it looked just like his home;
Whangara, which means Harbor of the Sun. Ruatapu, his
younger brother, would have killed Paikea if he had stayed
in Hawaiki; would have hit him on the head with a paddle
when their canoe filled with water. The whale saved Paikea
who was the whale. Paikea who saved himself.

9.
Aotearoa

Very like a whale . . .
—William Shakespeare, *Hamlet*,
Act III, Scene 2

Nga Kai o te Moana

SIMON SAYS THAT KAI IS the Maori word for food. A Maori woman from the Nga Puhi tribe stands with tribal elders from Waitangi Marae high up on a peninsula overlooking the Bay of Islands. In the mottled afternoon light her chin and lips seem stained with a suggestion of a moko.

The woman moves her hands with slow grace as she speaks to the small gathering before her. The land has changed since her youth, she says. She can no longer walk to the ocean, a few steps from the marae, and pick up green-lipped mussels, pipis, spiny kina and crabs. Her traditional food, mahinga kai, has been polluted from somewhere up the many tributaries that feed the bay. Even if there were no pollution, there are so many people now to feed on the small amount of land returned to the Maori people by the New Zealand government. She asks her iwi to impose taipure— no take—a traditional Maori conservation tactic, along the coastline to protect the ocean's treasure, nga kai o te moana.

'I am so hungry,' she whispers, 'for the food of my childhood,' and her hand rests sadly on her stomach.

One of the elders pats his huge round belly.

'If I still hunted for a living,' he chuckles, 'I wouldn't be this shape, eh?'

The other elders laugh.

I have a lot to learn about New Zealand, Simon says.

In the Volcano

Boswell: 'That, sir, was great fortitude of mind.'
Johnson: 'No, sir, stark insensibility.'
—James Boswell, *The Life of Samuel Johnson*

THE OCEAN LET US LIVE, and we sailed at last into the Hauraki Gulf. With a month of shore leave in New Zealand before the boat sailed for Easter Island, Nathalie was asked to depart—permanently—and agreed, reluctantly leaving the future collection of material intended for her PhD in Simon's hands. She decided to join a research boat in Australia, looking at reef fish. They were famous for having fabulous cuisine and a cook hired just to look after the scientists and crew.

I had put aside a vague intention of returning to Australia. Somewhere along the road I'd discovered I wanted to see the New Zealand Simon had described during our time at sea. I didn't want to miss Easter Island, didn't want to stay behind while Simon sailed on, but something had changed for me. Just going on wasn't enough. I disliked the thought of continuing on without Nathalie; knew I'd miss her knack for interesting trouble. Not sailing on felt like abandoning the children. The family gave me until the New Year to decide. A month of freedom.

Nat and I planned one last adventure together while Simon packed himself off to the South Island to help his friends finish their fieldwork. We took his car and went on a tiki tour south. Nat wanted to climb a volcano. When she ran out of time, she would take the train back to Auckland and I'd go on alone to the South Island. It felt good to be in control of our own time.

Tramping up snowy, windswept Ruapehu turned out to be oddly reminiscent of steamy Samoa and mudslides when in company with Shortstuff. At least this time Nathalie chose the perfect trail, flattish and winding up easily towards a double peak. There were no biting ants, no heavy brush to wade through. Each time we reached a goal, Nathalie set a new one, until it was obvious, she wanted to do the entire trail up to the caldera. I wasn't keen, although the landscape was a dramatic black and white and emerald, green, a soothing antithesis to eyes still squinting and bloodshot from the burnout blue of the open ocean.

I was limping after a few miles, from bad shoes and lack of muscle tone. Being aboard ship does nothing for one's physical endurance. I stopped and soaked a sore foot once, in an opaque-blue glacial stream pumping down from the peak like an open fire-hydrant. We finally agreed to go at least to the first, southern crater. I did want to look down into a volcano. I wanted to know for myself if one could, or could not, see the centre of the earth through these giant ventings. Aboard *Cachalot* I had dreamed about the roots of volcanoes, and tidal waves, and great white sharks. I told myself one had—perhaps—to face all these fears, eventually, in order to know oneself.

The fog cover was intense, though it eventually shifted, rolling like a huge blanket onto the higher peak to our right—or Nat would have had us up that one as well,

173

despite the warnings we'd heard of rotten ice. A hosteller had told us that two German women had been sucked under the ice into a river of melt only days before. Nathalie will always want to climb the highest peaks. Me, I'm as happy to look up as down.

We made it up to the snow line on the smaller peak and pulled out our map. The drawn trail skirted the crater itself, circling the lip of rock surrounding it, but what we saw before us were footprints and colored stakes leading straight out over a round snowfield. On the opposite side, the trail climbed steeply, leading presumably to a series of craters. We felt safe following the footprints. I didn't want to go up indefinitely, but I did want to get to the opposite rim and see what we could of the line of craters the map represented with dots marching across the range. So we walked out into the circular snowfield of the first volcanic crater.

Halfway across what was beginning to feel remarkably like a lake, I noticed that our footprints were turning a pale and tropical blue. Lakes are familiar to me; I know the signs for lakes; but who can tell the nature of a volcano?

'I don't like the look of this,' I remember saying, and I asked Nat to walk further away from me, so that if one of us went through the ice, the other might not. I remember having time to think that pulling up one of those long stakes might be a good idea, to hold sideways in case the ice broke.

'Do you know what to do if you fall through the ice?' I asked Nathalie, just before I fell through the ice.

I know I yelled. I had a vision from *Call of the Wild*,

running scenes through my mind: a sled falls through the ice, pulling all the dogs down with it—the greedy stupidity that leads the drivers to take chances. I didn't want to die. The bare second it took to fall was terrifying, hackle-raising. And then I was standing in ice water just to mid-thigh.

For a minute I was afraid to move, then I found I could brace my hands against the edge of the hole and step up to the surface.

'We are getting the hell out of here *now*!' I yelled, already running back the way we'd come. For once I got no argument out of the mountain junkie; she was too busy laughing. The ice water and slush packing my boots felt good on my swollen foot. I walloped Nat with a slushball once we were clear of the rotten snow. Halfway back down the trail she congratulated me on my effective method of getting her to turn around.

Beware the Nathalies of the world. They have no mercy when others have weaknesses. She left that night on the 1 a.m. train, boarding the Auckland express with a DB Draught in one hand and a Speights in the other.

It hardly seemed worth getting up the next morning. Rain and no little Swiss motivating dynamo. I wandered around town in a drizzle, finally booking a ticket for the ferry over to the South Island and Simon. It was going to take a while to get to Dunedin—Eden's Fortress—and I found myself suddenly in a hurry.

Fresh Bones

The aorta of a whale is larger in the bore than the
main pipe of the water-works at London Bridge,
and the water roaring in its passage through that
pipe is inferior in impetus and velocity to the
blood gushing from the whale's heart.
                                    —Paley's *Theology*

SIMON HAD AN IDEA. HE helped begin a campaign to
woo his New Zealand supervisors into sponsoring me to
design a research project of my own, on dolphins, if I
decided to stay behind when the boat sailed. He knew they
had some data available on the tiny Hector's dolphin,
endemic to New Zealand and at the opposite spectrum in
size and distribution to our giant sperm whales. I read every
science paper Simon had and approached his supervisors
with ideas proposing possible areas of study. A year of
research promised so much. It could be a step forward, allow
me to create my own direction. I wouldn't have to be the
Nanny anymore.

   Simon introduced me to an expatriate Canadian with
a big smile. She allowed us to help her with several dolphin
dissections that were meant to provide information on
population ecology and, eventually, toxin levels. It felt right
to be learning again, like striding freely on the beach after
our cramped months at sea.

ON A CEMENT PAD ON the seaside of the university aquarium, Sara the Canadian, Simon and I were dissecting two female dolphins. Like most of Sara's specimens, the first one had been a by-catch in a gill net. The fishermen had been trying to catch fish and only accidentally netted the young dolphin. You could see the marks where the nets had bitten deep into the struggling dolphin's flesh. Most of the by-catch seemed to be juvenile males. Possibly the adults were better at avoiding the death-traps. The fishermen were being surprisingly helpful in providing Sara with any dolphins they caught accidentally. Many professional fishermen were not happy about the gill-netting restrictions, which were meant to give some seasonal protection to the dolphins while they were near shore and too young to avoid the nets.

Sometimes Sara would hear about dead dolphins washed up on shore and would go and collect those as well. Occasionally they would show the same scarring from the nets, leading her to suspect that a few of the fishermen were getting rid of evidence instead of handing it over for study. Sara could still get the information she wanted, but it made for smelly, horrible days. The second female we were dissecting was a beach-cast specimen. She did not have any obvious net marks on her, but she was not fresh.

We opened up the netted female first and took measurements, removing teeth for ageing and ovaries for reproductive status. We were just in the process of flensing the bones in preparation to send them to the local museum when two groups of tourists came trooping through the area where we were working. The first was a young school group, who gathered around to stare. Their teacher expressed disgust at the blood and exposed flesh, but the children showed a keen interest.

'Why did you kill that fish?' one tiny girl-child demanded, launching Sara into a lecture on gillnetting and mammals. The teacher listened to that. The children just wanted to touch.

'No!' Sara's voice was sharp. 'We don't know for sure what killed any of these dolphins, and humans and dolphins are close enough to share many diseases.' She indicated her plastic gloves and butcher's apron.

The class moved on. A group of Japanese tourists gathered around.

A woman asked, 'Are you going to eat it?' The meat was a deep red and looked like the best cut in the market—if you ignored the smell. That was Simon's cue.

'No way!' He smiled to show he meant well. 'Most of these coastal species are loaded with toxins. Part of what we hope to learn is what kind of poisons these animals carry, how much their blubber stores, and whether their toxin load is affecting their breeding.'

The woman looked skeptical.

'Any animal high up on the food chain is going to have a greater percentage of stored poisons in its flesh,' Simon said carefully. 'It's called bioaccumulation. A concentration of any toxins in the lower species accumulates in the predator species at the top of the chain or food web. We are at the top of the web. If we feed on other animals, like

178

dolphins, which are also at the top, we get the megadoses of the toxins their bodies have stored. If toxins are affecting their breeding, it is likely to affect us as well.'

The woman didn't understand a word. Didn't want to. She frowned and walked away without speaking.

'Not the sharpest knife in the drawer, was she? I wasn't even *talking* about all that political hoo-ha around eating whale meat,' Simon said grumpily.

'Eating dolphin and whale is a touchy subject,' Sara said quietly. 'A lot of Japanese believe the Americans are campaigning against whaling to force the Japanese to buy American beef.'

We finished flensing and bagged and tagged the unrecognizable lumps of meat and bone that had been a dolphin.

It made for a long day, but the second female was already thawed so we started in on her. She was the beach-cast specimen, not as noisome as some but her skin looked strange and patchy. She looked even stranger inside.

'Look,' Sara said, 'her milk glands are full.' When they were pressed, milk spurted out.

We looked further. The mesentery, normally a clear, Gladwrap-like tissue holding the intestines in place, was beaded with yellow pearl chains of swollen lymph glands. Her immune system was highly activated.

'Oh,' Sara said sadly, 'look at this. I think she'd only just given birth.'

We looked at the still-inflated uterus.

'Could the calf survive without her?' I asked, knowing the answer.

'No.'

We finished as quickly as possible, feeling ill. It was disturbing to look at something so like one's own reproductive system, and so diseased. (Sara said most of the specimens she'd had before been juvenile males).

We took a long walk on the beach afterwards, none of us speaking, just breathing in the fresh smells of the sea. There was nothing but ocean between the cold sand beach where we stood and the Antarctic. The water had that look of wire-brushed steel. I felt decidedly queasy. I didn't like it. I was on land. I pictured the calf out there on its own, so young, and probably so briefly alive.

WE SPOTTED A FJORDLAND CRESTED PENGUIN— unusual here—and lay on the sand to watch it. It sat quietly against a sand dune and molted. A penguin molting looks something like a fat dustmop with ringworm: delightful.

'It's strange,' Sara said finally, 'how desperately important issues in one era are not even a question in the next. Today, you Americans can't decide whether to allow the morning-after pill to reduce teen abortions. Tomorrow, birth control may become mandatory around the world, and we could find ourselves fighting for our right to breed, if we still can.' She breathed out heavily. 'To me, the research being done on persistent organochlorines, endocrine disrupters, estrogenic compounds—all our dangerous garbage—completely overrides the emotional arguments of whether whaling should be allowed or not, or of whether one nation should have a say in what another nation eats. Putting aside all other environmental impacts, philosophical beliefs, political arguments, what-have-you, it is quite obvious that whale and dolphin are simply not safe for humans to eat.'

'It's a cosmic bloody joke,' Simon said. 'Here ya go targeting endangered critters for aphrodisiacal medicines, like as not. Where's the bleedin' logic in that? They wouldn't be endangered in the first place if they bred well, would they? Then the toxins they carry make us even less fertile. Brilliant aphrodisiac . . .'

'An argument for natural irony,' Sara said, waving towards the penguin, as if the odd, uncomfortable-looking bird illustrated her point.

'Or purposeful, bloody-minded ignorance,' Simon said, glaring at me for some reason.

Perhaps I'm beginning to understand what the grandmothers gave me all those months ago with their story about the last whale. How my babies will hate their parents when the oceans are bleak and rotting, like the carcasses of magnificent animals we can almost imagine on a black shore. We need to eat, we need to shit, and our garbage outstrips our imaginations and feeds our food. We can admire a whale, we can eat a whale, a whale can eat us, and we wish to continue eating the whale, living the whale, absorbing its strength into us. We will also die without everything that is and feeds the whale. The whales are dying from us.

But I finally know who my imaginary audience is while I'm out here, living these stories. It's my children.

'You're preaching to the converted,' I told them both.

Introduced Pests

We have met the enemy and he is us.
—Walt Kelly, *Pogo*

MATING AND THE SURVIVAL STRATEGIES of geckos seemed opaque until I started looking in the mirror. There I saw Ren and Stimpy, two young examples of their species, sitting on my hand, licking strawberry jam from my fingers. They licked their own large round eyes, goggled each other, and occasionally goggled me as well. Like many babies they had big heads, liquid eyes and stubby, foreshortened limbs. Their suckery finger pads gripped mine. When in a strange country, you get cuddles where you can.

I was looking after these two for a mate of Simon's in wildlife management who was off helping Simon with a week of fieldwork, studying young male sperm whales feeding off Kaikoura. I was missing out this time but getting interested in the other animals being studied by Simon's friends. At the moment it was geckos. I couldn't imagine giving them back.

The jewelled gecko, *Naultinus gemmeus*, is native to Otago and considered threatened, its numbers in gradual decline due to introduced pests. The Department of Conservation asked for volunteers to help clear gorse from an area in which geckos had been spotted. I'd been introduced only recently, but after staring into the moist, goggle eyes of Ren and Stimpy, I signed up for my first weekend of clearing gorse. We were to start the next morning.

183

I was cooing something sticky like, 'More jam, baby?' when I heard 'Can I do that?' from the doorway of Simon's tiny flat. My date for the zoology ball had snuck up the rickety stairs and was leaning against the doorframe as if he'd been there a while. Simon had asked Temuera to cover for him while he was in the field. I got the geckos; Tem got me. Tem was well over six-foot, black hair and beard, pointed eyebrows, dressed in motorcycle leathers. My mother's favourite nightmare. The gentlest thing about him was the lilting Kiwi accent.

I said something clever like, 'Oh. You want to hold them?'

'Nah., I want to lick your fingers,' Tem said. Great. I like to think Stimpy rolled a baleful eye. I eased the geckos gently onto their fern log and closed the top of the terrarium.

'So, what's the plan?' I said.

'Well, I'd like to get you into bed by midnight,' said my so-charming date.

'Remind me,' I said bitterly, 'why am I going to this dance with you?'

'Because your toy-boy's dumped you for a bachelor whale and you're embarrassed to show up *sans* date.'

'Said "boy" being your best mate. And that's what you're wearing?'

'I could take it off,' he said.

'Please, god, no,' was all I could manage.

Simon had first introduced his friend during a game of underwater hockey—the national sport after rugby, to hear them tell it. It's played with snorkeling gear, fins and mask, on the bottom of the pool with a heavy puck. Tem's team motto was, 'Short sticks, no balls.'

'Can you at least dance?' I asked as we walked out to his bike, starting to wish I could spend the evening in Simon's flat having nice jammy cuddles with the lizards.

'No, and I've got a short dick,' he said. That and the noise from his battered old Yamaha killed that conversation dead.

It didn't feel so awful, when we first walked into the crowded hall, to be with someone who belonged to the department. I wouldn't have gone by myself. I'd only been staying with Simon for a few weeks and already rumors were flying. I was becoming familiar with some of the students from volunteering as a fieldwork grunt. It was a rare way to learn the countryside. I really liked the people I'd worked with so far, but when grouped together the zoo department became a mire of gossipy 'sticky- beaks', according to Simon.

You wouldn't have thought folks who studied genetics could be so incestuous. Tem worked as a technician, creating and setting up the equipment used in many of the field studies. He was also working as liaison between several local Maori iwi and the university scientists on hunting and management issues.

He said it was a typical 'wildlife' ball. Women who looked tanned and capable in T-shirts and jeans seemed mousy in sacky nightgown dresses. Men who should have known better were getting by with sneakers and dress blazers that hadn't fitted since high school. Everyone smelled of mothballs or formaldehyde.

'Going for that Farmer-Don Johnson look,' Tem muttered.

My date, on the other hand, must have had lessons in basic slut-wear. Under the butch leather jacket he wore black jeans, black cowboy boots and a silk blouse that showed a few lush hints of chest hair. This guy had gallows shoulders as broad as the door. He looked great. He also knew it. He draped an arm across my shoulders as we walked into the room.

I shrugged him off. 'The rumors are going to be bad enough as it is.'

Tem winced. Across the room I could see one of the wildlife students from the old-school cadre, Trevor-the-Possum-Hunter, notice our arrival.

He headed over with an athletic Cary Grant mince. Trevor insinuated himself between Temuera and me, steering me away for 'a private wee chat'. He'd looked small, almost prim, next to Mr Underwater Hockey, captain of his team. I saw heads turning as we moved away from the door, some whispering starting, and a scattering of laughter. I'd stranded Tem in the doorway by himself, a black-clad obelisk in a room full of chattering monkeys.

'I am just concerned for your reputation,' Trevor whispered in my ear. 'You should know that dating the staff is just not done. Or rather, it is done, and then we all talk about you.'

His attention suddenly diverted, Trevor minced away again, leaving an odd feeling in my gut. What was that about? I walked across the long room to a glass case full of old museum specimens that was holding up the liquor bottles. Tem stood there with a beer in each hand, watching me do the long mile.

'Here.' He handed me a Steinlager.

'D'you wanna get out of here?'

'Nuh,' he said. 'I came here to dance.'

'You're kidding. This place is as dead as . . .' I pointed through the glass under the line of bottles, '. . . as dead as those. Christ, what are those?'

'Dead things,' he said. 'Dead and stuffed.'

I heard someone snicker nearby.

'They laughing at us?'

'Does it matter?'

'I don't like it.'

'Don't listen,' Temuera said, taking my arm and steering me into the middle of that huge, bright room.

'But no one's dancing yet.'

'Sod 'em,' he said. And we danced.

It was awful. How do you find your rhythm when you're spot-lit in a bright and empty space, sure that every other person in the room is watching you? But he wouldn't let me edge off the floor. And oh, how he danced. He pounded the floor with an angry, rhythmic stomp, laughed with a flirty hip wiggle, fluttered his hands like a Hawaiian maiden, flexed and twirled and sweated until, finally, my feet found their own rhythm and we danced together.

I had forgotten Trevor and the rest until I felt a warm hand on my shoulder. Tem ignored him and kept dancing, but I finally stopped. When I did, Tem just turned his back and walked away. Trevor stepped in before I could protest. He danced badly.

'Don't get involved with that guy,' he said between the huffling and the shuffling and the awkward little hops.

'Why?'

'He's dangerous.'

Temuera was shrugging on his motorcycle jacket and heading for the exit.

'Yeah, and what are you?' I asked.

'Harmless and slightly sleazy?' Trevor showed his gums. For a second, I almost liked him. Then I didn't. At all.

'Yes,' I said, 'that's it exactly,' and I left him there. It was like looking into those hungry, needy, baby gecko eyes, all warm and glistening—and they were begging me, begging the world to acknowledge them, validate them, tell them they existed and that their world was not becoming extinct. Geckos belong in New Zealand, are part of its heritage. I was becoming a deep believer in protecting unique wildlife, but this guy was just a lowlife. And I was an Introduced Pest.

I caught up with Temuera trying to start a cold engine in the parking lot. After a while he stopped trying to tell me to go back in there and face the crowd. I climbed aboard we ended up freezing our ears while we flew out along the river road and down Otago Peninsula. We spent the rest of the night talking on a cold, windy beach, looking out towards a welded-steel horizon that hid Antarctica. And then it was morning, and I'd promised to chop down gorse, and we were

188

already out there where the gorse was, so we found an open pub, had breakfast, and he came with me to do his bit to save the gecko.

There were geckos all through that gorse. The young wildlife managers were already scratched and bleeding by the time we arrived on the Yamaha. There seemed to be Rens and Stimpys everywhere, fleeing the tramping feet as the prickly gorse piled high.

'Are you sure these things are threatened?' my large friend asked an older man wearing a beige DOC uniform.

'Yip,' the man said. He seemed typical of the older generation of wildlife managers, silvered and weathered as a barn door. 'Nowhere else on the South Island you'll see so many.'

We stared at him.

'Is it in the realms of possibility that the geckos are here *because* of the gorse?' Temuera asked.

The man's face went red under silver over beige. 'I've spent me whole life battling noxious weeds,' he said, staring right at us. 'I've poisoned 'em, dug 'em up by the roots, burnt 'em, and still they come back. So don't try and tell me there's anything good about sodding gorse.'

'Well, it does have pretty flowers,' I said. We rode the motorcycle back to town.

'I guess introduced cats and stoats and things might not have much luck hunting through a great thorny bush like gorse,' I yelled over the rush of sea wind. Tem tapped his helmet to show he couldn't hear.

When we got back to the flat, I invited Tem inside to

warm up with a cuppa. Trevor's door flew open as we passed. Simon's flat was right above his. He stood half naked in the doorway, hairless chest rippling with smooth boy muscles, looking at me with those glistening eyes. Anyone could hear he had company.

'Perhaps we should talk,' Trevor said.

'Perhaps we should stop talking,' I said, and Temuera stomped his black boot heels extra hard as we walked up the stairs. Subtle.

Inside, I picked up the jam jar lying on its side. The window was open and papers from Simon's desk were scattered about. The lid had been pushed off the top of the terrarium and the fern log disarranged. A fat grey cat that often hung about the building was lying curled inside on the bare earth, licking her chops. Ren and Stimpy had failed to make the evolution awards.

Why Do Whales Beach Themselves?
Isn't Life Tough Enough?

(A brief exposition on life and sonar)

TRYING TO PUT MYSELF IN the head of a toothed whale, I imagine patterns of sound building pictures of the world, inside my head. Can this be so different from patterns of light? If your world is sound and light and pressure, can you send out a pulse through the liquid world to bounce off the more solid pieces in it, impacting and echoing back, stretching sound, squashing it into a sense of speed and direction, and firing more and more bursts into the void for information?

Perhaps patterns of sound look like the raised impressions made on a toy frame pierced by a thousand pins: when you place your hand underneath and push upwards, only the hundreds that touch the shape of your hand push back. Sartre could visualize sound and apparently it made him nauseous.

Imagine someone else firing the pulses of sound and you receiving their information. Sound and light are infinitely shareable. I eavesdropped on a conversation once and learned something that improved my situation (for a time).

What if the other human had intended me to hear but couldn't speak to me directly?

Supposedly an aboriginal tribe in southern Australia had conventions, formed by culture, where a woman was not allowed to talk to her husband's brother except through the medium of her children: 'Ask your uncle if he would like some food,' she might say, but what if the child was too small to repeat the words? Mightn't they be said aloud just the same, and to the same effect? And if a picture inserts itself upon the aural receptors of your brain, do you ignore it just because it wasn't created by you? Not if it is a picture of a big shark about to eat you and yours.

Perhaps this realm of bee-like group communication helps explain the incredible altruism we think we see (hear?) among dolphins, the whole pod rushing to the aid of a beached individual, often stranding the entire family group. If a voice screams for help inside your head, how do you know if it is your own or another's? And how can you resist?

If you speak the language, you reap the knowledge and assistance of a people (assuming you speak it without a bloody American accent, Simon says), become one of Us rather than a Them. Do dolphins hear us thrashing about in the deep the same way they hear their own people distressed by disease or pain? There was a pilot whale once who dragged a woman down fifteen meters by the leg and then dragged her back to the surface again, admonishing her for rubbing him inappropriately in a familiar area, the way he would admonish a calf who was out of line. And there are all the stories and myths of shipwrecked sailors brought to shore by unknown sea creatures.

How can we ever understand the workings of a mind in an alien environment—even when that environment is our own primal soup—when we can barely understand the accent, language, ideas of other humans who developed on land as we did? We all came from similar places, dolphins and humans, so perhaps understanding even a tiny fraction of how sea mammals communicate tells us a little more about ourselves.

And yet we romanticize them, and it clouds our understanding. Why do we need to find other creatures who speak as we do? Will it solve our own cosmic loneliness? And why are we also afraid of finding what we seek? It is pointless to ignore the patterns of communication that surround us every moment of every day: the birds whistling, the dogs barking, the dolphins echolocating and receiving images that any other might share. It is a simple thing to visit any farm and quickly pick up a few grunts, whinnies and squeals that will elicit responses from the animals who recognize them.

I leaned from the second-floor window in Simon's flat and let out a call I'd heard from a cat in heat. It brought three tomcats running over the roof in fewer than four minutes. If that's not interspecies communication (false lead though it may have been), what is?

Always with the questions, Simon complains.

Basking Shark

Impatient to assume the world,
I am moved by fancies that are curled
Around these images and cling:
The notion of some infinitely gentle
Infinitely suffering thing.

—T. S. Eliot, 'Preludes'

SARA-THE-DISSECTION-LADY CALLED for a hand with a basking shark beached under the climbing cliffs at Long Beach. We took her small utility truck; her friend Kasch-the-Dolphin-Dude and Simon and Temuera came along with heaps of knives and plastic bags, a measuring tape and a camera. We could smell the dead shark before we'd even reached the ocean side of the dunes.

At first, I thought I was seeing a long, low rock. It was huge – well over six meters. Up close, it looked like a theatre construction of a sea monster. There were holes in its sides where you could see the crisscross of fibrous muscle and shiny white cartilage, all covered with an elephantine grey burlap skin. The skin was wrinkled and sandpapery with millions of tiny 'teeth' called denticles. Even the seagulls had left it alone.

Humans hadn't, though. The dorsal fin, the pectoral fins and the tail were missing. Someone had hacked at the jaw. The stomach was everted through a tear under the dorsal fin. The fishermen who had caught the gentle monster in their net had taken its liver.

The gaping wounds showed a central railroad track of opaque porcelain cartilage. An eye was still there, although drained of fluid, and the brain, once exposed by Sara, was full of sand that had been pulled in by the collapsing jelly-filled canals of the shark's electromagnetic receptors—*ampullae de Lorenzi*, Sara said, excited to see proof of them in this species. They were long canals the width of a pencil. They showed externally as pits around the eyes and nose. They were part of the shark's navigational system. This shark had been beached at least a week.

It is likely that the basking shark had been caught in offshore nets, finned, gutted and released alive to float painfully and dying to this beach. Sara was furious that no one had told her sooner that it was here. Then at least she could have had a chance to make use of the corpse.

As it was, she discovered a few things. It did have electro-receptors. The brain was decomposed jelly, and nothing could be learned from it, so after Sara took a few measurements and pictures (explaining to some wrinkle-nosed rock climbers that this plankton-eating shark was harmless to humans), Temuera took a gardening machete and tried to cut a huge square in the metallic, elephantine skin. The heavy skin dulled his knife. It defied dissection. Tem and Simon had to stop and sharpen the blades.

The men tried holding back a square of skin attached to a huge, twenty-five-centimeter-thick layer of white muscle while Sara hacked away underneath with another blade. A thin layer of rich red muscle was exposed that looked similar to dolphin meat. The majority was a swirl of dense white meat as short-grained as that of swordfish. There was nothing inside the body cavity but a tube that looked like intestine. Where were the vitals?

They cut higher. The wind came up. Someone cut something that gushed a flood of watery brown liquid. It didn't smell too bad, considering the general atmosphere of rot. The men finally managed to remove several big squares of skin and muscle, which Sara and I dragged down the beach towards the water, and the red-legged gulls arrived in clouds.

More squares, and the black-backed gulls claimed the entire area, driving away the smaller red-legged gulls. The basking shark's insides seemed empty. Temuera started cutting into the thigh-thick circular pipe everyone assumed was an intestine. The tube had no inner cavity at all, although it smeared his knife with brown goo. It didn't smell like guts. The more he cut, the more the sides puffed out and expanded, filling the knife wound.

'This isn't a gut,' Tem said.

'What else could it be?' I asked.

He cut out an entire section, revealing a second, narrower, forearm-thick pipe behind the first, which gushed watery blood when he slashed it.

'It's a male,' Sara said. 'That big tube is one of the testes.'

'No way!' I said.

'There's no inner cavity,' she said. 'It has to be. The testes are in a similar position on dolphins.'

'Pretty impressive,' Simon said.

196

'Try and top that,' Sara said. 'It's at least a meter and a half long.'

'Right whales have testes weighing one metric ton,' I said, quoting from my reading. 'That's 1000 kilos. Biggest in the animal kingdom.'

The men looked impressed.

'For their body weight, I bet deep-sea lantern fish have bigger,' Tem said. 'Because they attach themselves to the female's circulatory system and their bodies atrophy until they are just gonads, really. Just swimming nuts.'

'What a waste,' I said, looking at the rich meat, the poor finned shark, the gigantic potential for procreation in a species considered, unofficially, to be in trouble.

Of course, they misunderstood what I meant.

Bird's Blood

It is not true that life is one damn thing after
another—it's one damn thing over and over.
                    —Edna St Vincent Millay

WE HIT A BIRD FLYING low across the road. I wasn't
driving, but my foot hit that imaginary brake as the bird
swooped down. Simon did brake, softly, expecting the
belated swerve upwards that came just a little too low, too
late. The bird bumped gently off the edge of the fender,
hardly noticeable unless you'd been watching and thinking
of the relative frailty of birds. I looked back and saw it
flopping in the road like a dirty rag. Simon pulled over. I hate
pain worse than death.

The bird was large and grey-brown. Its beak was
yellow and gushing blood. The wings flopped convulsively
until I picked it up and then it sat quietly in my cupped hands.
It seemed so calm I thought I could leave it in the grass, let it
live or die its own death. I wanted to not be part of its living
or dying.

'It's not going to make it,' I told Simon. Even minor
wounds seemed fatal to these feathery hollow bones. Puffy
feathers floated across the road.

'I can't kill it,' I said. 'Tell me what to do.'

'I could find a rock,' Simon offered.

'No.' I pictured hitting it again and again without
being sure it was dead, maybe causing more pain.

The bird sat quietly, panting blood. Everything

198

should be allowed its chance at life, I told myself. I put the bird in the long grass. It flopped over and beat its wings frantically. Its back was broken. I picked it up and it sat quietly again, panting. 'I don't want to do this!' I whined.

Simon offered to help, but I refused. I have always known I am a hypocrite. I eat what I refuse to kill. I can skin, cook and eat meat, as long as it's thoroughly dead. But I don't want some good-intentioned person putting me out of my misery no matter how I howl. Everything should be allowed its chance to live, to die, but death is better than pain when there is no hope of life. At least when it is an animal that cannot tell me otherwise. I think. Maybe. Is it?

I wrung the bird's neck, so afraid of botching the job I twisted its head off entirely, feeling the thin (warm) feathery skin slip off the bones and the vertebrae stretch and break under my fingers. I flung the body across the road, yelling. Then I was sitting in the car again, and Simon was wiping something off my neck with a tissue.

'Don't look,' he said. The feeling of fragile skin was warm in my hands. I didn't look. We continued out to the cliffs to help Temuera with his research chores, sticking our hands into little blue penguin burrows, hoping they weren't trampling their eggs from fear of us, banding and weighing them, recording new pairs, ducking when gulls dive-bombed us for walking too close to their nests. Hoping we weren't doing more harm than good.

Mental Floss & Boogie Boards

(In which I finally face fear & fail to boogie)

NIETZSCHE SAID: 'THAT WHICH DOES not kill us makes us stronger.'

But what if it doesn't? What if each terror and fearful near-death experience whittles one down to a toothpick? Leaves one scarred physically and spiritually timid and unwilling to face the next test?

I believe panic kills faster than—or as fast as—incompetence. My fears begin and finish with the ocean. It is such an all-encompassing, powerful entity. Simon taught me how to duck under the huge waves so that they passed overhead, rippling down the length of my body so it felt like seaweed rippling and snapping in a tidal pool. But then I tried stuffing myself into a tippy kayak, having just learned to roll it in the sterile environment of a chlorinated pool. In the big ocean surf, I felt the panic building before I even left the beach. I was used to getting into deep water from a boat. I didn't have experience with these huge crashing waves.

I sat through three waves hitting my tiny, borrowed boat as I pushed off from shore, my hands tingling and my mind screaming, 'Too big!' The fourth wave came at me like a nightmare of a tsunami. I'd given up before it even hit me in the chest and rolled me in a panic of bubbles—don't lose the boat, you have more time than you think—except it hit so hard did I remember to breathe and I can't get *out* arching away from the boat, remember the spray skirt got to pull it

200

off can't curl under and tumble over and over and suddenly something to push off from—the bottom? Still in the boat, my hands pushed me up out of the sandy froth while the waves tugged the boat and my legs seaward. I was in less than a meter of water.

A tiny boy ran up to me. 'Are you all right?'

'I'm new to this,' I gasped, a harsh sound that wanted to be a sob.

He kept asking. I climbed out of the kayak and stayed out, sitting on the shore, watching the tiny kids riding the waves like miniature seals. I was disgusted with myself but trying hard to decide whether I was just being stupid, trying to do something dangerous before I was ready.

Do I be smart and stay out? Do I be brave and try again and feel good afterwards? Or sit here and feel like a schmuck?

I got my brand-new boogie board out of the car's boot and tried that.

A wave came and got me again. I couldn't dive under the water with the buoyant board tugging at its tether. I tumbled and swallowed water, and trudged out again, disgusted with myself and deeply afraid to go back in.

The ocean was so large, and it took my body so completely against my will. I knew I had to roll with it, use the gigantic force that battered me to my advantage. But I was terrified, short of breath at the thought. I sat on the beach again and groused to myself. *Wimp.*

I tried a third time. This time with no boat, no board.

Just me. Just it. I body-surfed a tiny, shallow wave right up the beach. I quit while I was ahead.

At home, I found my back was sprained in two places. I finally know why people go to gyms. It's so controlled. Boring, but controlled. No fear. I have to go back out there, but it is going to be on a much calmer day.

I ALWAYS DREAM OF SHARKS when I am returning to the ocean after time away. Sometimes I can wake up just enough to turn the 'no, no, no' sideways wag of my pelagic fear, and force it into the 'yes, yes, yes' nodding smile of a dolphin. That is when black and white dreams turn to color.

Another State of Grace

(In which Temuera brings us home for Christmas with his mum)

GRACE IS A HARD WOMAN. Her face is tanned by an irresistible Southern Hemisphere sun that burns within minutes. She has the stocky, muscular body of an outdoorswoman. She's only half a century old, but her teeth have the bright white shine of glazed porcelain. I saw her grab at her mouth halfway through dinner, and then go picking through the roast, looking for the two front teeth that had broken away. She calmly tucked them back in her mouth but spent the next two days chasing after them when they escaped again.

I found them once in the sink, looking very much like chips from the pipi shells Tem and Simon had gathered at low tide for our tea. I think she liked me a little in that moment. She'd given up on the teeth at that point, thought they'd gone down the gurgler, she said, and her with her seventy-year-old 'bahstihd of a boyfriend' coming soon to share our meal. I had wanted to eat the shellfish raw until I saw those teeth shining wetly at me from the sink. Then I was happy enough when she made them into fritters. I'd never seen anyone do the work of opening shellfish while they were still alive. The pipis gripped onto life, their little dense white feet desperately trying to haul the two halves of their shells back together as she wedged them apart with a paring knife, one by one.

The fritters were delicious. The boyfriend, Stan, ate his share, complaining all the while that he didn't like pipis. Stan's teeth were whiter than Grace's, giving him a twinkly, boyish grin. She announced that she was going to see her friend Taffy to get a new set of teeth and ask him to make them even brighter. Temuera told us Taffy'd tried to convince her that the TV-star sparkle she fancied made his creations look fake.

'I had them all out when I was in my twenties,' Grace said. 'Best thing I ever did.' She was tucking the two front teeth back under her lip again.

'Don't they hurt?' I asked, eyeing my meal for the odd stray fang.

'Hurt a lot more before,' she said, 'when I was young.'

GRACE HAD A BOWLS TOURNAMENT the next morning, but we talked around the kitchen table most of the evening. She was three-time champion at the club, spending a lot of her time now she'd retired playing golf or fishing, gambling or playing bowls. In Stan, she'd finally found a partner who liked to do the things she did.

The problem, she said, was that Stan was a 'man's man'. He liked to go drinking with the boys and often didn't invite her along. Sometimes there were other women as well. It made her so mad, she dumped him at least twice a year, sometimes more, swearing she'd never take him back, but she always did. She wouldn't live in the same house with him anymore, though. Sold her house and moved to a smaller one so there wouldn't be room for him. He just went and

204

built his own house down the street and visited daily on his cherry-red scooter, his thick white shock of hair perfectly coiffed, rattling along on his way to the club, or stopping by afterwards for a meal and a list of his faults. She didn't spare him her opinion.

Grace didn't stay long with Temuera's father. Instead, in the early 1960s, when she was in her late teens, she took a boat to London and had her baby overseas—got her boy the prized British passport. She didn't bring him back to New Zealand until Tem was almost four, about the age at which her own biological mother had brought Grace and her baby brother to New Zealand after World War II. Grace's mother had given her children to these safe green islands, adopting them out separately before leaving for worn-out Europe again.

Grace had no idea where her birth brother was, or what their last name had been. She'd tried to find him, but the adoption records were incomplete, even after the laws changed and allowed her access. Grace was not interested in finding their mother. The older couple who'd raised her, her parents, didn't tell her she was adopted until she was thirty. But she'd known. Talking about it made her irritable.

'Tem got on better with the Wrinklies,' Grace said. They'd looked after him when Grace was working. Tem still missed his Nana. He took his grandparents' formal wedding and family photographs out of drawers and propped them about the house. When he wasn't looking, Grace put them back in the drawers.

NOT LONG AFTER RETURNING TO New Zealand with four-year-old Tem—who hadn't spoken a word yet— Grace married a Maori fisherman from Nga Puhi. He had three sons already, all of whom Grace raised as her own. Later, he and Grace had two children together: Sanna, her only girl, and Pipi, named for the small shellfish his mother peeled so expertly, and which her husband adored.

Tem's stepdaddy knew he was dying before Pipi was born. A wasting disease rotted his circulation, his legs, and left him an amputee.

'Dying in the living room for years,' Tem said. 'The smell was horrible . . .' Two of the boys eventually went back to their other mother, but the eldest chose to stay with Grace.

'I don't give away my children,' she told us around the dinner table that first night, nursing her glass of bourbon. I asked how she'd managed. I couldn't imagine how she'd fed them all, even along New Zealand's fertile coastline.

'Didn't always. We ate so much fish the boys got anemic,' she said. 'The visiting doc had all the kids collecting puha greens from the side of the road for the iron. Tem won't touch it now.' Even poorer relations from the whanau showed up at her door for extended vacations. She also said, with a terrible casualness, that she'd left her husband several times when he'd beaten her, but that she'd had to return because she'd no choice.

'Mainly because he cried,' she said to us, her grown daughter, Sanna, listening avidly. 'No one believes me when I tell them that. Oh, he was a handsome devil.'

206

AFTER DINNER TEM AND I tucked his nieces into their cots and told them a bedtime story. When the girls were settled, Simon washed and I dried the dishes while Tem sat down to talk to his mum. I'd spent most of my life traveling, doing whatever I felt like, really. I'd often wondered what it would be like to have a child, a life partner. I got lost in watching Tem and his mother talk in the next room, in thinking about these people I was just getting to know, whose features peeped from the little girls' faces, manifested in their lashes, their skin tone. Those sleeping girls had looked so lovely to me, like watching crystal-clear star fields on a cold night.

The Hui

GRACE TAKES US OUT TO the local marae the next night.

Before we enter, Grace sings the karanga as we walk up to the meeting hall, her voice rough from years of smoking. She giggles a little as she grates out the words:

Karanga mai, karanga mai, karanga mai.

A singer answers back from the hall in a high clear wail.

I walk at the head of the group, next to Grace. We stop outside the front of the building where there are chairs waiting for us. I'm told women are expected to sit towards the back. Grace sits where she pleases.

The building is decorated with grimacing carvings applied like veneer over aluminum siding. Behind the building, on slightly lower ground, the spire of a Catholic church peeps over the high wooden walls, making its presence known. A large man named Geoffrey introduces himself as a teacher of te reo taonga, the treasured language. He stands and makes a long speech in Maori.

'This is a forum where all may speak,' another elder, a woman, interprets for us.

'This is the place where any issue may be raised by anyone, male or female, and be heard. In the beginning, Tane created the first woman from red earth and breathed life into her. So now, and again when you leave, we will all hongi. In this way, all bad feelings and hard words will be left behind.'

208

Someone behind me jokes, *sotto voce*, that in some versions of the myth, breathing wasn't the only way Tane brought the first woman to life.

We troop past to touch foreheads and rub noses with the elders, sharing breath. The hongi is a surprisingly soft caress. We go into the hall. Inside, Geoffrey welcomes us again, everyone standing together. After explaining the basic rules of the marae (no shoes on the mat, no bums on the pillows or tables, leave anytime you want if nature calls —even when an elder is speaking—fall asleep if you get bored), Geoffrey cheerfully exempts us from anything that doesn't feel comfortable, all in the name of good feelings and communication.

He raises his story stick and tells us we are going to spend the weekend introducing ourselves and our most colorful ancestors, singing, telling stories, talking about the Pakeha translation of the Treaty of Waitangi and the Maori version, and how the two differ. Later we will sleep where we are now standing. So we gather in a big semicircle, keeping our shoes on because of the cold, and never leaving to pee when a good storyteller is talking, because it feels criminal to miss it.

The Taniwha

NIGHT CREEPS INTO THE GREAT hall and we are each given a mat to sleep on: men on one side of the hall, women on the other. Grace tucks the little girls between Sanna and me, and we whisper while the people line up for sleep. The murmur of voices dies down. I am in a light doze when I feel a hand on my arm. I've been dreaming of taniwha the size of express trains, rumbling in and out of dark holes in the church; tearing strips of aluminum from its sides as they exit. I am finally, unhappily, awake but the noise doesn't go away.

'Is that Simon, you reckon?' Sanna's voice in the darkness. All the men are on the south side of the hall. The single, giant snore coming from that southern end is incredible. I can hear a rising wave of snickering and whispering the entire length of the blackness.

'Drop a sock in his mouth,' I say sleepily, wishing she'd left me dreaming.
The noise continues. It's like nothing I've ever heard in my life.

The taniwha whines like a steam kettle coming to a head, then just when it should bubble over, the whistling, whining gurgle hesitates. It stops. It chokes. The hairs rise on my neck, waiting for it to continue. There is no rhyme to it; the very arrhythmic tempo is part of why it is such a distressing sound. When it does boil over, the gasping, sucking lurch of bubbling pressure is so loud, it defies human origin. Again a halt, a terrifying suspense of sound, relief as the whine rises again. There is no chance of sleep.

210

It sounds as if someone is dying in the dark.

Sanna gets up and goes into the kitchen, where a few drinkers are determinedly breaking the marae rules on alcohol. She returns, and we listen in the dark to the taniwha dying. A tipsy elder comes giggling into the hall. He stands in the light of the doorway, yells 'Hey!' and claps his hands loudly. The taniwha stops doing whatever it is doing. The door closes and there is silence. A long, dark and waiting silence. When the taniwha starts again it is almost a relief. No one tries to wake him again.

I hear several people discussing dragging their mats outside and sleeping under the cold sky. Finally, four large men shuffle through the dark and drag the giant sleeper, shaped like a humped turtle in the dim light, along with his even greater snores, out into an anteroom, mat and all, where his sleep demons are muffled by the door once they slam it shut. The dark hall erupts into laughter.

AFTER THAT, I STILL CAN'T sleep. I can see the sleeping forms of the little girls cuddled into Sanna's side, and I feel a restlessness in me that has nothing to do with snoring gods and demons. Simon is just one of the dark, sleeping lumps on the other side of the hall. I get up and slip through the door leading to the kitchen, to make a cup of tea. The lights are on, and Tem is sitting at a table with Grace and a bottle of bourbon. We are the only ones awake. Tem is pale and wide-eyed. Grace is drooped over a glass, her tired face in shadow. I join them, and Tem snaps a photograph down in front of me like a playing card.

'Who's that?' he asks, voice abrupt.

It takes me a minute to adjust. It must be family photo album time again.

'Oh, that's you . . .' I start to say, then hesitate, looking closer. 'I don't know—who is it?'

'No. You don't know who that is,' he says and pours another glass. He's silent for a moment.

'I have a new brother,' Tem says finally.

There seem to be a lot of brothers already, between Grace's mob and the children from Tem's biological father. Tem's statement is not particularly shocking after a weekend of genealogy stories. I try to think of a tactful way to ask which side of the family.

'Read the letters first,' Grace says, from her dark corner.

'He's Mum's,' Tem says.

'Read the letters.'

'Is it okay?' I ask Grace.

'I'll explain after you read them.' She doesn't look up. 'It's time people knew.'

I don't like bourbon, but I take the glass Tem offers and reach more tentatively for the first of three letters postmarked from Britain.

'April 1966 is a date that means something to both of us,' the first letter starts. Now I'm startled. Tem was born just the year before.

I'm not writing because I want anything from you, and I will understand if you don't want to write back, but I want you to know that I've had a happy life and I love my adoptive parents. I want to thank you for adopting me out. I'm not interested in getting in touch with my father, who I understand did wrong by you. But I've always known I was adopted and ...I want to know you.

It is a very kind letter. Later letters, spread out across the last six months, talk about how happy he is that she answered. He describes his life, asks about hers. He knows a lot about Grace's family. He is a traveller. He sounds . . . nice.

'He must work for the FBI,' Grace says gruffly, 'to track me through two name changes and to know so much about the kids.'

I can't help thinking about what Grace said the first day we arrived, two days and a lifetime ago—'I don't give away my children'—and about all the children she took on and raised as her own: six children, eight grandchildren, some biologically related, some not: it made no difference to her, family was everything.

And yet in thirty-four years Grace hadn't told a single one of them about this baby she'd had and adopted out in England, one year after her first son was born and when she couldn't have been much more than twenty.

'Are you okay with this?' I ask her again.

'That's what all the kids have been asking me today,'

she says proudly. 'The first thing Sanna and Tem both said was, am I okay.'

'You didn't have the choice of abortion back then, did you?' I ask, and she shakes her head.

'No.'

'Have you ever told anyone about this before?'

'No. I'll tell you the story once you finish the letters.'

SHE WAS NINETEEN, ON HER own in a foreign country. Tem's birth had lost her a job as midwife at a London hospital. She went to work on a farm to have a roof over their heads. The farm manager saw the child as proof of Grace's 'loose skirts'. She held out for months, she tells us, while he 'tried to get into me knickers', this fifty-something matriarch with the sun wrinkles and the false teeth, hunched over her bourbon. Her eyes are in shadow, watching her younger self panic.

Finally, the man threatened her with eviction if she didn't have sex with him. Grace has a photograph in her album of baby Tem wrapped in blankets, lying on one of the huge fallen stones that make up Stonehenge. He looks like a sacrifice, swaddled white on grey stone over brilliant green grass. There is a blurred male figure moving out of the picture. That was the day, she tells us, when she gave in. Afterwards it got much, much worse.

'Did you ever have any kind of a real relationship with the guy?'

Grace shakes her head, wiping her eyes. 'I don't remember much of that year,' she says. 'He really tried to get

214

me kicked out after that. I took the baby and moved to a little shack on the edge of the property, miles from anywhere. It was so cold, I had to take the mats up off the floor to cover us, me and both the babies, once Matthew was born.

'I knew from the start I couldn't keep them both, but the agency didn't take Matthew right away. It was their policy. I took him home with me. It was hard when they came to get him. I don't remember.'

And Temuera didn't talk until he was four, and Grace had all her teeth out because they hurt her so. A terrible secret shutting both their mouths.

THE AUTHOR OF THE LETTERS, no longer named Matthew, wrote that he knew Grace had cared for him, because the social workers had done for him what no one had done for Grace when she was adopted out. They had let him read all the letters she wrote to the agency, desperately trying to find out how he was, whether he'd found a home.

Whether she could get him back, I hear in my own head, echoing across thirty-four years of silence. Thirty-four years of time going by, days filling up, and other children needing her.

'Are you mad at me?' Grace asks her son, as we all get up to break the spell and get on with the rituals of nightfall and the necessity of sleeping.

'I'm angry for you,' he says.

'I'm impressed by you,' I say.

'I love you,' Tem says quietly, looking into her face, hugging her close.

TEM AND I WALK OUTSIDE and look up at the night sky, needing to breathe deep. The snoring taniwha is still rumbling behind us, a muffled storm, but the sky is clear. I can see the Southern Cross and the Magellanic Clouds; small, irregular galaxies dwarfed by distance and time into puffs and swirls of light, satellites to our own galaxy. I think about my own travels and choices. I would never have seen these stars if I'd followed any path other than the one I did. But no one will ever reach out to me, when I am done adventuring, to tell me they are a part of me. That they want to know me.

   We all live life hard—is there another way? But Grace was young at a time when women paid for being independent. I tell myself that women were allowed to make a few mistakes by the time I got out in the world. I'd never had to be quite so alone, fight so hard, never had to stay in an abusive relationship for the sake of my children. Never had to give up someone I loved so much it hurt for more than three decades. So why are the cold stars blurring? And whose tears are these?

A WOMAN'S PREROGATIVE AT A traditional hui, Grace says, is that at any time, no matter how heated the debate or exalted the speaker, she has the power to stop all discussion and say:

   Ke te waita, ke te wai—stop talking and sing!

Swimming with Hector

(Upokohue, the puffing pig)

> Loveliness unfathomable, as ever lover saw in
> his young bride's eye!—Tell me not of thy
> teeth-tiered sharks, and thy kidnapping
> cannibal ways. Let faith oust fact; let fancy oust
> memory; I look deep down and do believe.
> —Herman Melville, *Moby-Dick*

ON NEW YEAR'S DAY WE were only slightly hung over
and determined to get out on the water because it was a
beautiful sunny morning, because *Cachalot* had decided
not to sail away just yet, and because we weren't sure how
much time we had left. I was still trying to make up my mind
whether to stay or go. When the boat sailed, Simon would
sail with it.

Kasch-the-Dolphin-Dude drove Simon, Temuera
and me out into the caldera bay of the old Banks Peninsula
volcano. The boat was a little aluminum-hulled Kiwi craft,
maybe fifteen feet long or less. Kasch was doing his PhD on
the dolphins' behavioral ecology, with Simon's
supervisors. I had seen many Hector's dolphins over the
last few weeks of the year just ended, all of them dead. All
beach-cast or caught incidentally in the gill nets that
Simon's friends had worked so hard to get banned from the
peninsula during the breeding/feeding season when the
dolphins came in close to shore. I wanted desperately to

217

see live dolphins. Just to make sure they were still out there.

'You may see them only from a distance,' Kasch warned, 'or not at all.
Don't be disappointed . . .'

They were there, though, right in the middle of the bay. Simon said even his supervisors had never observed what we saw that day.

Highly unusual behavior, Kasch wrote in his log. Hector's dolphins are known for being shy.

A female was spy-hopping: her entire head coming out of the water to the top of her pectoral fin and more. There was a thrashing of water and fins and tails all around her. We knew she was a female because she came right up beside the boat and presented her genitals to the air. We also knew there were many males thrashing and jostling her because they were leaping out of the water with pink dangly bits bright in the sunlight.

Kasch murmured something about how unusual this milling behavior was and cut the engine. We watched for two solid hours. Other boats full of weekenders came and went, their children leaning out and patting the dolphins as they slid and rolled past the boats. We took as many ID photos as we could and then leaned out of the boat ourselves, just watching. The female came to our bow and looked up at me, less than half a meter away, with the tiredest brown eye I had ever seen. Simon trailed a hand in the water and stroked a dolphin that seemed to be presenting its side just for petting. When he looked up his eyes were shining.

'They don't usually do this,' Kasch muttered. 'I don't think I brought enough film.'

'Can we swim with them?' Temuera asked.

'I don't want to encourage the tourists,' Kasch said conscientiously, 'but I'd really like to know whether they would change their behaviour around swimmers.'

The tourists left. There we were, alone in the ocean with a thrashing pod of spy-hopping, leaping dolphins crashing and bashing into one another. They had hardly shifted from their original coordinates.

Simon took the wheel while Kasch reloaded his cameras and Tem stripped down for a swim.

'Can I go in too?' I asked, just to be polite, assuming so, even though I was surprised Kasch was going to let us in at all.

'I don't think you are strong enough to get back in over the side of the boat,' Kasch said.

'Don't be stupid,' I said and started pulling off my clothes. None of the men stopped me.

The water would have been cold in a wetsuit. Tem and I both left our knickers on, out of some kind of false modesty. After all, we were getting into the broken and sea-filled caldera of a volcano to swim with mating dolphins.

Their behavior changed instantly. They stopped crashing and milling and began to move away. One thing I have found useless is to try to outswim a dolphin. I didn't swim after them; I just frog-kicked away from the boat, gently, with no speed or splashing.

There is a theory that dolphins will more readily approach women swimmers than men, possibly because of some unspecified body language.

Temuera was one of those big parsnip-shaped guys, and he had a powerful crawl stroke; he was probably trying to stay warm. He said later he saw lots of round dorsal fins receding in the distance.

I had no idea where the dolphins were once I hit that freezing water, but I forced myself to move along slowly, gasping for breath from the cold. Something brushed against my legs, and I panicked quietly for a second. It is an eerie thing to be touched by the unseen. I balled up, arms hugging my knees, and floated. A dolphin came up beside me. It brushed my side and flicked away. Twice—they had touched me twice!

When the female spy-hopped next to me, she looked directly into my face. I could see every crease and fold around that tired brown eye. As she sank back down in the water, I reached out my hands and stroked down both her sides. Perhaps, after two hours of being bashed by males, she was desensitized to touch, but she neither started nor flicked away. I moved along beside her with several of the males for what must have been only a short time. They flicked around my legs, staying near.

Finally, I noticed several boats, tourists, far off but moving towards us. I changed my angle back toward our boat, and instantly the dolphins were gone, not a dorsal fin at the surface. Suddenly I felt terribly alone.

TEMUERA AND I ARRIVED BACK at the boat at the same time, both half frozen and hardly aware of it. As I struggled to get over the high gunwale (rather feebly, I admit—it was cold!).

Simon grabbed me by the armpits and heaved while Tem pushed from below. I landed ungracefully on my face in the bottom of the boat.

The water instantly began boiling with dolphins again.

What the Nanny Said
(Dreaming dolphins)

SPERM WHALES AND HECTOR'S DOLPHINS are in the same order of toothed whales or *Odontoceti*. Sperm whales are the largest of that order, at up to eighteen meters in length. Hector's dolphins are the smallest in the world at a maximum of 1.2 to 1.62 meters.

Both types of cetaceans use echolocation clicks to navigate and to communicate. Sperm whales were once found in all the oceans of the world. Hector's dolphins are found only in the coastal waters of New Zealand.

One of their Maori names is upokohue or puffing pig. They are dove-grey and black and white. They do not have the bottlenose that the more familiar grey *Tursiops* have. The black of their pectoral fins runs into the black mask of their heads, which curve sleekly as a pharaoh's nose down to mouths underlined in white. Their backs and sides are the pinky grey of a rainy sunrise, and their bellies are pearl white.

They're usually shy and reserved, although they will approach small boats in groups of three to eight for short periods of time, usually leaving if people get in the water. They have a funny rounded dorsal fin—black—without the sharp scimitar crescent of the dusky dolphin or the bottlenose dolphin. They are beautiful. They are alive.

> The only thing that makes life possible is permanent, intolerable uncertainty: not knowing what comes next.
> —Ursula K. Le Guin, *Left Hand of Darkness*

222

Do Teardrops Fall Counterclockwise in the Southern Hemisphere?

Paikea was the whale. The Whale was Paikea.
—Robyn Kahukiwa

I HAVE NEVER RIDDEN THE whale. In another time, we swam belly to belly with giant sea turtles under the full moon as they circled their sandy sleeping places, watched the alert and curious stingrays play hopscotch through the long sea grasses and circled the feeding sharks jealously guarding their patch of coral. In dreams, we waver through the bull kelp with the rolling silk scarf of the octopus tumbling in the surge, twisting and spinning with the ever-changing glitter of minnows evading the long barracuda.

I've corkscrewed through bath-like waters of warmer seas and trilled to mother dolphins and their calves while they tolerated my play. I have stung my hands on fire coral and soothed them with healing mucus of brain coral. I have felt the tug of the sperm whale diving deep into the cold Pacific trenches and seen his speckled mouth gaping like a friendly dog's. In another place, I held his giant child in my arms while it died in a stagnant pool far from the sea and its mother, felt it crying while I cried. We followed whales to Aotearoa where Orion stands on his head, and felt welcomed by the friendly, brown-eyed smile of tiny black-and-grey dolphins. I have heard them singing, each to each. I do not think they sang to me. But I have known the ocean in my belly, its seaweed tendrils in my mind, and I am Paikea too.

223

The Greening

We have lingered in the chambers of the sea,
By sea-girls wreathed with seaweed red and
brown, Till human voices wake us, and we drown.
                    —T. S. Eliot,
                    "The Love Song of J. Alfred Prufrock"

Temuera at Ten

THERE'S A MOGGY IN THE HOLE. But no—moggies
are fat and furpurring, and this one's all pinclaws and hiss.
Tem sees the sun tilt into a dark burrow and green eyes slit
and glow. Green like Daddy's fish-hook necklace. Tem is
learning the difference between house moggies and fierce
bird-killers. He has poked his gatherstick into every burrow
on the fishy-smelling clifftop and not a squawk or beak rattle
answered. All are empty.

Sad seabirds, adult shearwaters, circle high, gullets
stuffed with fish for their empty houses. Tem's belly
rumbles: none of their fat muttonbird chicks left for Daddy's
table either. He imagines last year's pile of greasy smoked
birds outside Daddy's crib, the wee holiday cabin they use
just for food-gathering on the cliffs of the South Island. A
special trip south with Daddy each year. He can taste the
almost nauseating heavy air around the door, like fish oil and
sea spray. 'Flying fish,' Daddy jokes, 'be digging flying fish
outta the ground, boy. No muttonbird this year, but.'

Tem stabs his gatherstick into the hole—here Puss
Puss—hears the whine of fierce moggy rise up into the air
over empty nest mounds, piercing the air like a siren calling
the dark parents until they circle thick above. How could all
those meaty shearwater chicks be gone? He pushes down
into earth, feels it edge past the soft stopper of moggy. The
cat's whine rises and shatters into growl. The stick kicks in
Tem's hand. Tooth marks, he bets.

Easing the stick past the soft and teeth, he begins to

pry. No back door in a muttonbird nest—why should they? Who's to run from but Tem and his daddy, who never took more than would die in summer from ocean-blooms when they colored red? Or big bull sea lions yanking the chicks under, squawking and beak clapping, folding up like a snotted hanky tugged quick underwater and disappearing forever? Too young to know better, too young to know— then gone. Daddy says that to Tem, now and again. But Tem is the one still coming here, when all the rest have gone their own ways. Here until all the muttonbirds are gone and the sun is going too.

'Don't you stay until the dark,' Daddy said, 'and if you do, don't you nevah chase a bird downhill.'

Tem pries and pries at the hungry cat in the seabird's nest. The sun angles low over the hills, just high enough to reach the breeding grounds: clifftop plucked bare of green, all roots and dark earth spotted with birdshit and burrows and piles of nest dirt. Wide beams of light gold each burrow, then slant down to water, burrows turning gold to grey then black. Tem is at the last one. Hunching knees to chest, he pries the green-eyed moggy from its last meal with his gatherstick.

No muttonbird for tea tonight. The sun glows in the cat's green eyes and Tem watches them slit. Moggy's cry spirals, and the parents of the eaten one's circle, the rustling of wings becoming huge as the sun squats down, nestling like an enormous egg on the hilltop. A light feathertip brushes his cheek, and the moggy quick stops its high whistle and goes flat. A stoat couldn't be so smooth and flat

226

to the ground. The cat's eyes tilt up towards something, some cool darkness behind Tem's neck. He tucks his chin to one shoulder, peers down along the dark bow of cliff behind him, curving down to a sheer drop. The plucked earth is dotted with statues: each nest mound, each dead burrow, marked now with a thin bird; upright, staring, adult shearwaters, quiet as herons, wings folded, crowds of narrow watchers, stone towers with black eyes, prickling the fur on his neck. He startles, gives a last great shove at the moggy, and it darts out of the hole like a stray breeze; claws caress him as it leaps, three soft lines through the fabric of his trousers.

Tem sits down quickly onto dirt, a bare pruned circle of nesting earth. The burrow is meters from the thick golden tussock grass that moggy scrambles towards. The cat banks around staring birds, careening like a billiard ball, somehow no closer to the grasses than just before. Moggy bounds downhill. Not chasin' birds—downhill, Daddy, downhill— no, bein' chased towards nothin', to the drop, bitter edge of the landworld. The cat rears back, claws up; flat black silhouette against sun-struck water, a huge red sun pouring into the hills behind. Now the sun is pouring out, pouring down, a creeping river of gold ahead, under red, under purple behind. Silent watchers stalk forward one pace, another. Wings fan out; the ripping of sails beats a sudden wind, and the final curved shell of the horizon reflects its last light onto the ocean: bright busted yolk. Tem sees a flare, an afterthought, of spark—green eyes—and sun and moggy disappear together over earth's edge.

Taniwha Dreaming

'TANEY-FA' GOT NO SHAPE, DADDY teases the boys. Taniwha is old green moss and stone. Don't wanna cross him. Older than the gods in the upturned canoe that made the mountains. Gods climbed out onto the rounded canoe bottom, upside down in the Great Southern Ocean, and froze into the western peaks, iced gods in the rocks of an island canoe. The taniwha were there first . . . maybe one turned that boat. Maybe taniwha don't like humans, those new mammals, fast-toothed hunters that eat the old balance away, eat the trees, eat the birds that have always walked through green island mist. Maybe taniwha *don't* hate outsiders wrecking their island boat.

You wanna find out? No nice ending to meeting with a taniwha: you do something bad, you do something good, it's the same. Maybe they get you, maybe not. No reason, no moral story. Taniwha is when the wind blows up for no reason, when ground breaks and hot mud sucks you under, when waves peak in the middle, when pastures buckle and earth slides. When birds cry out in human voices and humans scream like birds. Maybe taniwha make things green again, old and green. Greenstone carvings—tiki spirits and fish-hooks—moss-green feathers, old bones, and yellow-green eyes of witches (even they scared of the taniwha). Aotearoa been old green, young green, since the landboat set sail from its mother with the first birds, before mammals were born, before humans dreamed of monsters. Don't meet with a taniwha. Don't you dream him.

Simon at Twenty

SIMON IS ON THE SOUTHERN cliffs. Chasing birds. His eyes look at things differently since going to university, since his travels around the world. Tem's daddy is long dead and far away north; the holiday crib burst its planks in the winter rains. Simon smells the oily grease of stacked muttonbirds and feels a ghost nod to him from the swaying leatherwood sapling growing between rotting steps. 'Too young to know better,' the wind says; 'too young to stay.' Simon feels cold shivers up both arms. He and Tem returned to the South Island to help protect the shearwaters and the new colony of royal albatross on the bay side of the steep headlands where Tem and Daddy gathered muttonbird more than a decade before.

Albatross have their own pedestaled nests covered in white guano. From the channel, their nesting ground is a tapestry of knobs and hollows. A hand brushing over it would feel flexible knots like the knobbles on a woman's hairbrush. Simon's girl has long sunburned hair. She's coming to meet him from the city, is thinking of sailing north with him. 'Couldn't you have stayed?' whispers the wind. She'll join him soon. They need to talk.

The biggest birds are soaring up there in the dark over Simon's head, each wingspan wider than Simon is tall; the smaller shearwaters loop around the albatross like terriers following the pack leader. Tem's daddy would never have imagined the albatross vanishing. Just eighty birds are left in the new protected colony. There are nine nestlings this season, sitting fuzzed and plump, fatter than the adults: so fat, if they fell over, they'd lie there until Simon set them upright like bowled pins, careful of his eyes near those forearm-long beaks. 'Putting a little back where it belongs,' Simon says, and Daddy's ghost nods and flaps its leaves like empty gums. No one would be hunting their kai in the adjacent shearwater colonies this year, nor next, and Simon's traps should protect both the albatross and shearwater chicks from the predatory mammals encroaching on an island evolved just for birds.

SIMON SHIVERS AGAIN BECAUSE HE'S on the cliffs at night, hearing ghosts, but he can't hear the biggest birds riding the soft air currents. He's listening hard for something. His headlamp drills a thin hole through the dark to make circles where his banding kit lies spilled in clumped tussock grass. He showed Temuera the traps that first morning, after offering his respects to Daddy's ghost at the busted crib. Simon found Tem laying out a feed of big green tidewater mussels to dry under the grasses where the birds wouldn't find them.

'Good kai,' the older man grinned, dark hazel eyes stitched about with laugh lines and the wind.

'No muttonbird though, Tem; none yet, none here, right?'

Temuera's smile went still and quiet. 'You tellin' me, boy? I know what taipure means—so did you before you became some Pakeha scientist. You can say 'No take' if you want. Reckon it's the same thing, eh?'

230

'Reckon so.'

But Simon worried. He worried while Temuera helped him set the ferret and stoat traps all around the albatross colony, laughing with him over the big stuffed albatross behind glass, meant as a sop for the tourists who weren't allowed to hassle living birds. It was wide-winged, crucified on a copper post, its ice-white body as big as his torso, its eye as big and deep and dark as Temuera's, the beak an orange spear dipped in red.

'Got a wee prezzie for ya, bro.' Temuera was reaching into his sack.

Simon saw the greenstone fishhook swinging at Tem's throat, skin-oiled over the years until it had turned darkest greeny black. When Tem and Simon were boys, Daddy had said this pounamu held his mana. Wouldn't let them touch it, touch his soul, though it swung and glittered and was fine.

'Kai for me?' Simon asked.

Temuera missed the greasy, satisfying glut of muttonbird so bad, it woke him sometimes at night with a hunger deep as grief. 'Eh, that's a good one, Si,' he said, 'Kai for you. The new kai. Kentucky Fried Kai.'

Tem pulled a cat out of his bag. It was a big black cat, stiff and harsh-haired, its eyes dried and lightless. The red line of a collar peeped through the clumped fur. It was flat as roadkill.

'I caught him near your nests, mate. Pretty good, eh? I kill 'em where I find 'em. You can count on me, brother.' He swung the cat at Simon, who leapt, almost falling.

231

"'S'matter, boy? Cat got ya tongue?' Temuera hooted.

'Jeesus, Tem, ya basta'd, you know I can't touch those things—and look, anyway, that was somebody's pet moggy.'

'I'd like to smack them with the same four-b'-two,' Temuera said, all serious. 'No right bringing the murdering bastards onto these islands in the first place. You wish I'd left it to nosh on those great overstuffed chicks?'

'No, no. Yer not wrong; I just don't deal well with cats.'

'Oh, crikey dick, you're a worry, mate. You a superstitious Pakeha now? This your job, ain't it?'

'Introduced pests, yeh.'

'Good-oh. Moggy, meet Simon; Simon—ya dag—meet Moggy.
Simon's a scientist now, Moggy, he's gonna eradicate yer arse. Good word, eradi-cat.' Temuera looked into the cat's dead eyes. 'Now yer all introduced, and you can get on with it.'

'I'm not thick, Temo, I know me job.'

'Reckon ya better, mate, 'cause these birds ain't out of the hole yet,' and Temuera laughed.

SIMON SITS ALONE ON THE cliffs now, in the dark, the long-dead moggy winding its tail around his ankles with the cold puffs of wind off water. Six of his nine albatross chicks are dead. Temuera almost dead himself from the news—all that work, all those hopeful generations gone with one ferret's lung-piercing teeth. Not killing for food, this one,

232

but killing and killing because that's its nature. The birds, protected too long on their ocean-girdled island, their defenses soft, placid on the ground, have no recourse but flight and the seabird chicks are too young and fat for that. 'Too young to know . . .' Daddy's ghost whispers.

'Don't you mean too old?' Simon shouts suddenly, to no one—to the grieving wind. 'This place is so old, no one can live in it!' Pleistocene forests—they'd named the strangeness for him at varsity—terrible old land with its iced and belching volcano sides and giant tree-fern stumps, the shades of huge flightless birds tramping through the bush like misshapen deer, tiny bird-mice scuffling in the leaf litter and mossy owl things stomping on thick legs up mountainsides because why fly when mammals are still undreamed of? Marsupials unheard of. Humans nothing but a nightmare in dark-bellied canoes.

The wind doesn't answer, and the headlamp spears through the dark onto Simon's boots. Seabirds glide overhead in the dark. These had at least the defense of flight, and the sheer-sided islands protected them a little with abrupt cliffs and shifting winds. Aotearoa had been the first to cut away from Pangea, a liferaft for flightless birds and big insects and a very few small, dinosaur-like reptiles. Its own ancient tribes filled every niche with the first, unique shapes while the rest of the world's crowded house fought and changed and bred sharper teeth, sleeker forms, meaner and more efficient ways of eating, of killing.

The albatross knew the world; they'd seen it all. They were the planet gliders, taking off as soon as their fuzz-fat bellies sleekened to scaled feathers. One tip off the pedestal and over the cliff edge they went, gliding on four-metre wingspans that caught every puff of breathless sea air. They soared for months, for years, things of the air and the tense bowed edge between water and sky, never touching down on the toothed earth until they came home again, seeing everything from their smooth height, touching not a thing but water and air.

But now the rest of the world had come to them, followed them home with killing red eyes. The lovely grey and brown shearwaters, cutting circles, measuring and patting the huge wave-tips with a feather's edge, were children, playing while the grave dark eyes of the albatross gyred above, watching time pass them by. Tonight their cries sounded like human voices, startling Simon from his circle of light, calling 'No, no. No, no,' in the high night air.

SIMON BREATHES DEEP AND COLLECTS his banding kit: fishy-smelling burlap bag spilling over with colored tags and measures. Tem caught the ferret. Caught *a* ferret. Nothing left but a bloody rag. They had traps around the entire perimeter, but once the killers learned the taste of ancient meat, there was no controlling their appetites. An aerial poison-drop might help, but he despairs for the remaining chicks. He's heard rumors the poison strangles more than small mammals, and the local iwi are against it. Simon licks his lips. He yearned for that meat taste again himself, felt the same hollowness inside: it never goes away.

He is on the cliffs at night banding muttonbirds—

234

sooty shearwater chicks, he reminds himself: bird, not food name. Band them, weigh them, count them. Nothing would be left now without humans interfering. So he's been taught at university, far from this cliffside in a smoky city.

So he believes. So he doubts in the greenstone-tinged depths of his soul.

'Remember, boy,' whispers the wind. He finds himself wondering why he ever wanted to leave these islands.

THE *WAK-AK* OF AN ADULT shearwater breaks his thrall to the pinpoint light, and he picks up his sack to follow the cliff's edge towards the nesting grounds. The albatross colony fades behind him with all its lovely, lost whiteness. Oddly enough, the shearwater colony up ahead sounds just as it did two decades before. There is a cheerful, busy fussing and flapping, such a populous sound of feeding and squabbling he tears up from ghosts of memories that were never his—the hunt, pecking battles, proud scars, stacks of oily meat.

Someone smokes by the crib, telling the old stories of Maori gods and tricksters—monster taniwha, bigger than the deer-high moa, all gone now, ancient, unpredictable, uncaring, bird-gods, and birds! Such birds flapping overhead: the sky is dark with kai. Grease runs down his chin and he has the full-belly feeling of a good feed by a sweat-warm fire.

Simon comes to the end of the tussock grass and almost turns and runs back in stomach-clenching shock. The nesting grounds are barren. Nothing has greened the

235

black earth in a fistful of years. Corroding piles of dirt, spotted with old shit and empty burrows, crater a moonscape of dead earth and twisted roots. A grave silence damps the air from any sound of wind or wing. Nothing living, nothing dead.

Nothing at all.

NEVER STAY OUT IN THE dark, the wind says, the dark wind says, the dark, and if you do . . .

A BIRD STARTLES UP OUT of the tussock grass at his feet, shoots up into the air and Simon leaps after it, the hunter in his belly bounding after its kai. Downhill, the wind says, and he sees the nothingness suddenly beneath him, feels the cold black behind the tussock. Never run downhill, the wind says, and he twists about like a cat in midair, grabbing at the long golden-haired grasses lit up by his headlamp, shadowing the nothingness behind him, catching the harsh cutting slices in his hands, feeling them glide through his fingers, stomach lifting as he falls, the long scroll of the tussock feathering past his middle, his face, his hands, and then no, they call no, no, far above, the watchers in the dark air; no, no and down into velvet, down and down, nothing left, nothing there, nothing at all but the smooth black silk of black air and a crazy whirling pinpoint of light hurtling down; never downhill after birds, Daddy's sad voice whispers, 'less you want to fly.

I'm flying, Daddy, Simon thinks. I'm flying into black, and his mind grips hold of that, holds on hard until the

236

dark rises up to slap him in the face, slapping down, rocking back his head, back with a cold heavy force that crushes the air from his chest, dragging the bag still looped in his hand, shoves and pulls him into a sack with no air, struggling bodies stacked together tight, squeezed into water, and throws him back up again; a breath.

Another.

A shaking circle of light throws a plank of water in his eyes. He drops the bag. He kicks off the things that still pull him down into where the dark is so dense, he cannot take those wheezing sucks of air, can't see; he throws the glasses away (were they water-spotted? No matter). The light is still burning. He struggles in the web of his clothing, molts it into the freezing water where it coils around him like weed. He is high in the air—sees the lit circle of cliff face, a wall of black ahead. He is low in a trough—a world of grey water. The taniwha who tricked him toys with him for a while and then grows weary of the game, sees the hint of green in his eyes flare then fade to dark, and throws him at the cliff with a wet, heavy claw.

There is one place up the cliff where the last of the yellow-eyed penguins leave the water, hopping in long lines at dusk. The trail follows a long sloping buttress, next to the only place where the rocky cliffs are undercut, leaving solid air between clifftop and water-top. A fine place to fall. The crumbling path beside the drop is one place where Simon can use his second life, given a chance. He smacks into the rocky buttress and the heavy-bladed kelp slips under his hands, tangles his legs, and he tastes the salt, his own salt,

237

and tumbles down.

The wet has him again, throws him from its highest peak, a thing to be ejected, a poison, a human. He hits a ledge, scrabbles with icy clubbed paws against slippery rock, nothing to grip, nothing . . . The water teases, pulls him back, draws him down with a weighted insistence, on his back, head dangling over the edge, one foot wedged in the rocks and twisting painfully—but it holds.

You have the length of one wave's roller, Simon. There is not another round of luck tonight. It is coming back to get you, Simon . . . and he hears his own voice calling, 'No, no. No. No,' in the high night air.

Trickster

THE KETTLE IS ON THE boil; I'm baking scones for the hunters' midnight tea. Not missing the warmth of them as yet, except in a comfortable forward-looking way, next to a fern-log fire glowing golden on ancient rimu walls. The knock is a heavy rumble, the thunder of a growing storm. I open the door and it's almost morning. I can't remember the time passing, but there is an odd grey-green light under long clouds silhouetted against a verdant sky.

Temuera is standing in the open doorway, looking huge and black outside the warmth of the wee crib. Tem is carrying something naked and white, with wings outspread: a grown albatross knocked from the sky and drenched by an early shower. Its solid whiteness looks so cold and lost. I feel my soul contract into a breath.

'Bring him in,' I say. 'For gods sake, bring him in.' And Tem steps across the threshold, carrying his burden into the red warmth of the firelit room, and together we shut the door against a colder, older light.

Epilogue

First Woman

Let faith oust fact; let fancy oust memory...
—Starbuck, *Moby-Dick*

IT IS WINTER IN THE Northern Hemisphere, but we are
still in summer. I put down my journals and notebooks and
turn off the lamp. The sun is drowning in the dusk of rolling
New Zealand hills that almost block our view of the ocean. I
call to my new husband to bring the meal he's cooking into
the living room so we can catch the world news on telly. He
stops on the way to pat my enormous belly.

'Who's your daddy?' he says to you, little taniwha, as
I groan our way into a big, soft easy chair.

We are going to name you Lilith.

On a low kauri table by his feet, Tem lays out a feed
of giant green-lipped mussels he's steamed with garlic and
wild rice.

'Good kai,' he says, and grins.

Notes on Research

This is the end of the whaleroad and the whale
Who spewed Nantucket bones on the thrashed swell
And stirred the troubled waters to whirlpools . . .

—Robert Lowell,
'The Quaker Graveyard in Nantucket'

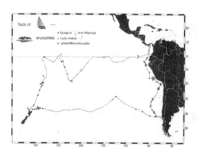

*Track of the
Research Vessel &
Sperm Whale
Encounters, 1992–
1993*

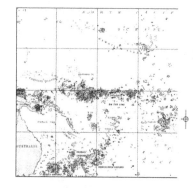

*Map Based on
Townsend Chart of
Sperm Whale*

THE SPERM WHALE DISTRIBUTION that we observed
in the South Pacific in 1992–93 has much in common with
the distribution of the 19th-century sperm whale catches

244

(Townsend, 1935). High densities of sperm whales were found along the west coast of South America, 'On the Line' between Christmas Island and the Phoenix Islands, along the Tonga archipelago and on the 'Vasquez Ground'.

However, only a single sperm whale was heard on the 'Offshore Ground' and the 'On the Line Ground' between the Galápagos and Marquesas. This last result was very unexpected, as high densities of sperm whales were known to inhabit this area year-round during the last century. No obvious explanation could be found.

—Dr Nathalie Jaquet et al, 1996

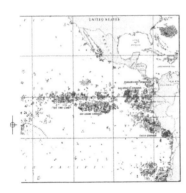

Kills along the Line, 1761–1920

* * *

THE NONINVASIVE RESEARCH conducted in the South Pacific in 1992–93 showed fewer sperm whales than expected, given the decade they'd had to recover their numbers since the whaling moratorium, instituted in 1982, and even taking into consideration a legal phase-out period that allowed some limited whaling until 1986. In 1994 rumors abounded of a number of countries 'taking' whales throughout the moratorium. That year the University of Auckland's Professor of Molecular Ecology and Evolution, Dr Scott Baker (who with his team developed the one of the first field-tests for DNA fingerprinting), first reported samples of multiple protected species being sold for human consumption in several Asian marketplaces. Among them were blue whale, fin whale, bowhead, right whale and humpback whale.

Truth, Lies and Food

I TRAVELED THE WHALE ROAD A SECOND TIME in the writing of this book. Along the way I pondered the vagaries of memory, the revealed truths made clear by every story told in the world, and the lies inherent in the very process of writing down any memory.

And what if I had written that Simon the accident-prone sailor had survived his fall from the cliff? That he sailed on with the boat and then flew home, following his own whale road, his *Hwaelweg*, around the world like the albatross? That Nathalie got her doctorate and organized her own whale studies, resulting in the long-awaited insight: 'Now I know what the Captain go through'? That the Captain's Wife later fought a good fight to motivate the whale research community about the US Navy's underwater sound tests, whose high decibels are rumored to disrupt fishes' swim bladders and deafen whales? That the Captain was and remains one of the most respected whale researchers in the world? That I know perfectly well who the father of my children is; and that he is imperfect and well-loved? And that in the effort to tell a true thing, I experimented with all the fictional devices I had ever read or been taught in order to feel a tale truly.

Would you believe me?

And if I then said, 'But the science is true', does that detract from other truths? And what about the way science is 'true'? There is an old joke about a statistician looking for a job. The interviewer asks her to define the meaning of pi and the statistician shuts the door and whispers, 'What do you want it to be?'

Science once defined one large male sperm whale and many females as a patriarchal bull with his harem (with all the human baggage that goes along with that metaphor). Our researchers watched in a different way, and saw a matriarchy visited by lone males. Once upon a time we saw dolphin pairs as the ultimate moral/romantic symbol of mating for life. Now we believe dolphins to be promiscuous, often pairing with a same-sex best friend who helps with birthing and rearing young.

Science has its fads (remember margarine and saccharine?), and ways of storytelling change with time as well, with every story experienced uniquely by each reader. We use memory, and story, and science, and no doubt religion, to figure out where we came from and where we are going. There may never be true or correct answers, but the journey informs our quality of life, our survival and our self-awareness (that thing we pride ourselves on as a species).

Currently our science tells us we are killing off multiple species unsustainably, and that many organisms are being adversely affected by pollution and damaged habitats. Perhaps we need to reassess our own human story: put ourselves back in the context of the world as an important strand in a complicated web, with drives that often rule our behavior. I believe this internal view can help us as a species to know ourselves, to protect our own environment with its complex and important diversity, and ultimately to help us save ourselves.

248

Then we can dream of our children living happily ever after—or at least as best they can.

What to Do About It All from Cradle to Grave

Two Toxin Maps:
*Ran*dom

Samples from
Literature of DDT
(top) and PCB (bottom)

Levels µg/g in Marine Mammal blubber 1993

—from D. K. McCutchen Thesis: "DDT & PCBs Found in Hector's Dolphin, Compared to Recorded Levels Across Several Species in Literature."

MY THESIS REVIEWED 100 PUBLISHED research papers from 1979 to 1993. The work did not attempt to cover all available literature or all species, and it should be noted that toxin levels found in internal organs would be expected to be significantly lower than those found in blubber. The thesis addressed the persistent organochlorines DDT (dichlorodiphenyl trichloroethane)

—the wonder-pesticide—and its metabolite DDE, and PCBs (polychlorinated biphenyls)—used in making adhesives, paints and coolants in electrical transformers. Amounts are recorded in micrograms per gram (µg/g) of toxin to blubber. Since these substances are synthetic, none would occur naturally in animals or humans. New Zealand has banned the use of DDT and PCBs, and a government decree demanded that all PCBs be located and destroyed by 1994. Unfortunately, due to their nature, this does not mean they ceased to exist.

Even though these toxins have been restricted in use worldwide, they are obviously pervasive and ubiquitous, probably crossing the equator from more highly industrialized countries. It was frustrating to find that researchers were often not collecting their data in comparable ways and, partly because of that and a lack of baseline data, physical effects from these levels were often un-provable. We were not willing to advocate difficult and possibly damaging experimentation on already distressed populations of Hector's dolphin (for example) to obtain these proofs, though several seal studies were included by virtue of experimental designs not possible for cetaceans. However, from the toxins' measurable effects on biological organisms from the cellular level up, it is now widely acknowledged that people eating whale meat polluted with hormone-mimicking pollutants such as organochlorines (and others) are, like all mammals, at high risk of lowered sperm motility, uterine occlusions, endometriosis, spontaneously aborted fetuses, bladder cancers, breast cancer (in men and women), testicular cancers, congenitally deformed genitalia, and other severe unpleasantness. These ubiquitous pollutants are sometimes being equated with chemical castration.

With a relatively small percentage of the existing total of organochlorines having reached the ocean so far (from dumped transformers and the like), effects have been recorded at every level in the ecosystem, from suppression of photosynthesis in phytoplankton to reduced fertility in fish.

New Zealand biologists have long recommended requiring manufacturers to take responsibility for the environmental chemicals they create, as an obvious deterrent to creating problems in the first place. Toxic chemicals must be monitored from cradle to grave. Fines for contamination should be concurrent with, and used for, cost of clean-up and reparation of the environment that was damaged. Public participation is crucial. In general, the mandate for all manufacturers should be that nothing is created that cannot be disposed of without causing harm. With the creator should ride the burden of proof.

It seems reasonable also to attempt the reduction of other impacts, such as overfishing and whaling, until toxins can be controlled, and more is known of marine animals' (and our own) survival capabilities.

We have known about these problems for a very long time. The toxin accumulation reported in more than a few research papers suggests that even if all whaling were

252

stopped tomorrow, the future of many slow-breeding whale species would remain in doubt.

But it couldn't hurt.

* * *

And indeed there will be time . . .
To prepare a face to meet the faces that you meet;
There will be time to murder and create . . .

Time for you and time for me,
And time yet for a hundred indecisions
And for a hundred visions and revisions
Before the taking of toast and tea...

—T.S. Eliot, ' *The Love Song*
of J. Alfred Prufrock '

Updates

POST WHALE ROAD, I WORKED A SUMMER on the Atlantic Coast with the Right Whale Gang on conservation of Right Whales (as-in the "right" whale for whalers to kill). The RW Gang was out of the Anderson Cabot Center for Ocean Life, part of the New England Aquarium (NEA), with their own field station in Lubec, Maine.

The RW Gang has a groundbreaking collaboration between researchers and non-researchers like big shipping companies (whose vessels accidentally strike RWs) and fishermen. For decades, the Gang has held RW Consortium meetings providing research updates to stakeholders and discussing RW conservation. Through these efforts, vessel speed restrictions were implemented, and shipping lanes shifted to reduce risk in high-use RW areas. Fishermen were inspired to create their own breakaway ropes and nets and have tested on-demand fishing gear to stem the frequent entanglements RWs face. Finally, some long needed government policy changes are upcoming that will hopefully turn around the whale population decline documented since 2010 and witnessed long before that.

The Woods Hole Oceanographic Institute (whoi.edu) posted online in 2022:

"The North Atlantic right whale is one of the most endangered whales in the world—approximately 360 remain."

254

AMY KNOWLTON, Captain of RV Nereid, Senior Scientist, Anderson Cabot Center for Ocean Life, NEA, wrote:

Aug 11, 2022

No research effort this year in the Bay of Fun-dy (BOF). In 2020 we saw no right whales at all in Lubec - first time this has happened in 41 years of effort in the BOF. A single new mom & calf were observed in 2021.

A team is up in the Gulf of St Lawrence now finding Right Whales (RW) in collaboration with a Canadian team doing oceanography. RWs continue to struggle but the Feds are finally stepping up their game with proposed protection measures.

HAL WHITEHEAD, PhD, Captain of RV Balaena & Lead Researcher, Dalhousie University, wrote:

August 29, 2022

We continue sperm whale research, particularly interested in cultural transmission in sperm whales. Luke Rendell and I describe it in "The Cultural Lives of Whales and Dolphins" University Chicago Press.

A culmination of studies and ideas started with our 1992-1993 voyage around the Pacific, is forthcoming in Proceedings of the U.S. National Academy of Sciences, "Symbolic marking in non-human cultures: evidence from sperm whale clans" by Taylor Hersh et al.

I saw Simon at the Scientific Committee of the International Whaling Commission about ten years ago, representing Australia. He was clear, to the point, and unexpectedly forceful in confronting pro-whalers.

The kids still sail, sometimes skippering our Research Vessel. Ben is an officer in the Canadian Navy now. Steff is a professional sailor and high-school science teacher in England.

Whale Winds

At Sea in the Bay of Fun with the Right Whale Gang

Between the Coast and the end of the world is why we are here.
Because here be monsters.

Bay of Fundy, Lubec, Maine, September 20, 1996

LUBEC IS DYING. There are no fish left. The lovely old,
paint-peeling houses are for sale because the fishing families
can't feed their children anymore and are leaving. Stores on
Main Street are boarded up, sometimes burnt-out by
desperately bored and angry teens. The R. J. Peacock fish-
packing plant is the only cannery still operating, seagulls
lining its roof like vultures. We see the rare tuna out there
in the bay, but the draggers ruined the shallows for bottom
feeders. Fishermen group together on tuna boats, working
for free in hopes that just one fish will bring in enough to pay
the bills. There aren't many lobstermen left. A few go after
whelks and a few more for sea urchins. No local will eat that
stuff.

On the road into town there's a weathered sign
reading: "Easternmost Point in Maine." Teens at the local
Red & White will tell you, like a litany, "Lubec ain't the end
of the world, but you can see it from here." And we do see it,
looking out from town toward the immense Bay of Fundy
guarded by thirty-foot tides and whirlpools named "the Old
Sow," and her numerous "Piglets." Between the coast and
the end of the world is what we're here for. Here be monsters.

257

Hurricane coming. Last week of field research and we can't get out on the water. From the cliffs overlooking the giant rip called Quoddy Road, the waves are spectacular, sheeting into the air like monstrous island-long whales blowing, atomizing the ocean after a planet-deep dive. The storm whips so fiercely Rox's dog, Stretch, is half windborne, ears sailing out from side to side like airfoils.

Looming out of the driving horizontal rain, New England Aquarium's field lab is a weathered land Leviathan, a stacked maze of rooms overhung by steep slanted roofs bearing up solidly under the assault. Inside, the chill is dissipated by the buttery fragrance of popped corn, the hum of computers, and a landlocked crew murmuring over newly arrived slides of the right whales we're here to study. Light tables glow. Keyboards tap.

North Atlantic right whales were once so numerous the sea was black from Georgia to Fundy during migrations along the New England coast. They're baleen whales, filtering tiny copepods in vast quantities from what are now, sadly, the same fast currents used as shipping lanes. Even a fifty-ton right whale won't do well in a collision with a tanker.

Vessel strikes, entanglements in fishing gear, and polluted food seem to be finishing the job the Basque whalers started a thousand years ago when they targeted these whales, so rich in oil they were called "oil-butts" and became commercially extinct in the twentieth century. The few left were protected from hunting since 1935. Today, instead of whales feeding across the horizon, one can see humans sitting in a staggered line stretching along the research lab's long workroom, feeding information about the few remaining North Atlantic right whales into luminous blue computer screens.

The stormy fringes of Hurricane Fran stopped all work out on the water. The town dock is empty of fishing boats, even the seagulls scattered away into the gale. Our research vessel, Nereid, is moored in safer harbor over in Eastport. Phil zipped over in the Zodiac to check her lines and came back wringing stormwater from his sleeves. Amy's been on the cliffs with Stretch, taking a break from computers and the incessant search to quantify the living and forestall the dying of whales. The wind sucked the air from her lungs and she sails breathlessly back into the lab, flushed with the exhilaration of the storm. Scott's on the phone, explaining how weather holds precedence over disappointed film crews. His daughters Brenna and Keely start combing the dog in the middle of the lab floor and arguing about the best way to eat Oreo cookies.

Jennifer and Carolyn sit and trade insults while re-inventing the world on computer, creating models of the bay and whale track lines. Martie bends earnestly over a light table, sorting slides, a cockatiel on one shoulder nibbling her ear. Lisa's going through files, regaling us with raucous inside stories on whale politics. Marilyn spread corrections of her aerial survey sheets over the kitchen table, keeping company with Rox who's painting Admiral's tail flukes stirring the wall above the stove. More than one ship called in a dead right whale floating tail-up in the bay, but it was always Admiral, our mad matriarch, who loves to stand on her head and stir the air with her tail. She's the only whale I can identify from a mile away. Phil knows them all.

I ask Phil to help ID a whale from video clips I'm organizing. Moe and Chris debate methods for re-fletching arrows used for darting and satellite tagging. Everything being done around the huge old house has something to do with right whales. The right whales to kill that are almost no more. Giant, blubbery, buoyant, knob headed, comb-toothed, North Atlantic right whales. There may be fewer than three hundred left; their numbers dropping. We are on the brink of an irreversible act, to save or lose this other species, so unlike us. I've read about these whales, dreamed them rolling in their giant tides. But with the arrival of Fran it's clear our time is running out. Field season is nearing its end with bad weather ruling out everything but indoor work, data analysis, and lab repair.

But the winds shift to a kindlier direction and Phil invents a plan to get us back on the water. Some crew will go south to Bar Harbor where Moe found a vessel to survey Brown's Bank, another RW habitat. I'm envious, thinking of sights I'll miss. But a day on the Nereid is worth gold now. The party leaves and we few go out to see what effect Fran had on Fundy, our Bay of Fun, and on the right whales.

I fully expect not to see a single whale my last day. I'm as relaxed as I've ever been on Nereid, knowing it's the end of something that may never repeat. I thought I'd already had my perfect moment.

The fog is thick. Sounds reduce; the slosh and creak of the boat is muffled—the water unnaturally still. With no

260

horizon we might be sitting on a pond. We're still feeling the effects of the storm. No one cares what happens next. The mist forces us to exist in each quiet, eternal moment as if that's all there is. We play whale roulette with the fog and just keep going.

"I think we should try over here," Marilyn insists, moving us from one identically opaque spot to the next, keeping us out longer than would normally seem reasonable, considering we can see about fifty yards or less. But then a pod of white-sided dolphins move with quiet puffs of breath through our circle of calm. And then, "I think we should be over there." Marilyn insists again and we're all so relaxed we go on and on, leapfrogging through fog. I fall asleep, only to wake to the familiar calls of "What frame are you shooting?" "Was that whale broken or continuous?" "Does it have lips?"—whale researchers identifying whales from the island-like callosities on their heads. I sit up to a new day of bright sun, not a single wispy shred of fog left to smooth the waters now animated by whales.

I grab a template to draw the identifying patterns of white callosities on black whale skin. Callosities are categorized as "broken" or "continuous" islands and peninsulas, scattered in individual configurations around each whales' upper jaw and lips, like islands on a sea chart. My drawing of "Broken, Two-Islands left," will later help us organize photographs and match this whale—using callosities like fingerprints—to the catalog of known whales. We record her presence and behavior in this time and place, leaving her unnamed for now, moving on to the next.

Rox spots a whale breaching on the horizon and other whales arrowing toward it. It looks like a courtship group is about to form. Phil's intention is to move toward the breaching whale, but we're on the same tack as the converging whales and are drawn, as if by whatever force draws them, toward a sight Phil says has never been observed in all the years the Project has been monitoring right whales in the Bay of Fundy.

First, we stop to photograph a mother and calf we haven't seen before, excited that they might be new to the Bay. We're all focused on documenting the pair, but then look up to a stunning sight. In a full circle around the boat, in water so calm you can see entire whale bodies below the surface, there are twenty right whales skim feeding, open mouthed. A single basking shark moves among them, its triangular dorsal fin a giant billboard. Some whales are feeding in formation, a staggered line of dark heads moving together through the blue-green surface. I'm frantically trying to video until Phil quietly tells me I'm missing the sight of a lifetime. I take the camera away from my eye and really look. We're surrounded by a quiet whirlpool of whales. They're no longer the lovely sleek animals we've seen playing and courting, but suddenly sea-monsters at a glassy table, creating new ocean wavelets with huge open mouths. Wide gums show slick above baleen plates overlapping as heavily as wet feathers. Stocky tails pump forward like pistons. Eyes peer sideways from jutting chameleon-like cones where one expects sockets. For the first time I can see the whole whale and not just what shows when they surface to breathe. That may be the one thing our species have in common after all. We both breathe air.

I suddenly understand the odd sea-monster drawings in the whaling museums. I see creatures I'm just beginning to recognize as individuals—Mavynne and Knottyhead, Kleenex, Punctuation, the high-spirited Admiral, our tail-stirrer—and they've become incomprehensible beings simply by opening their mouths. Long baleen plates are tucked into a lower jaw almost separated from each side of the head, leaving a wide triangle open in the front where water streams in, filters through baleen, and rushes back out over curved lips.

"Now I know why their tails are so big!" Marilyn says softly, "They gotta be incredibly powerful to push that mass of water forward, like dragging a bucket over the side when the boat's moving."

The double blowhole of the nearest whale snaps shut after a bubbling rumble. It sinks and we can see the entire pattern of head callosities laid out beneath the water like our templates. The head swells back to a bulbous body covered in fungoidal circles like a moss agate, body shorter, flukes wider than I imagined, after seeing them only in parts. The entire crew is hanging open mouthed over the railing. Not a single camera shutter is snapping. We sit with whales feeding for hours. How can we possibly know what it is like to be them?

In the end we stop all pretense of work, cut the motor, drop a hydrophone over the side, and listen to the moans and groans of feeding. The sun sets. In the dim light we continue handing the headphones back and forth, sitting dead in the water, not even attempting to follow when the group finally drifts gently away from us, still feeding.

As the moans grow fainter, I take a moment alone at the bow, rocking and listening to the first and last sounds I'll ever know of right whales. The forceful, shushing, trumpeting sigh of breathing on every horizon.

...

There have been calving booms and droughts since 1996, but vessel strikes and entanglements have been the primary factors keeping right whale numbers down to around 392 known individuals at Phil's 2006 count, 360 in 2022. The RW Gang worked toward changing shipping lanes, helping vessels avoid whales with aerial surveys and acoustic warning systems, and attempting to develop whale-safe fishing gear. They've instituted yearly North Atlantic Right Whale Consortiums open to every discipline that impacts or studies these whales. Incorporating multiple disciplines makes them a landmark in joining advocacy and research. One hopeful theory is that preventing the deaths of even two mothers a year could turn the population around.

Then, December 2006, Marilyn wrote that Admiral, the grand old dame of the Bay of Fun, became entangled in fishing gear. Admiral, first photographed in 1979, age unknown, was big and old and strong. She was boss of the fleet, tail sailor, identifiable from miles off as she waved her flukes at the sky. Always biggest, healthiest, most exuberant,

Admiral got free of the ropes that left deep wounds on her peduncle and fluke. Entanglement didn't kill her outright. But, Marilyn wrote that she looked unhealthy and was failing. As I grieve for playful Admiral and hope for her survival, she somehow personalizes a great sadness for all the less known creatures and species disappearing in this century of drastic change. We've all shared air.

In 2022 Amy wrote:

> All the whales you mention in 1996 are now gone. Mavynne suffered a nasty entanglement and eventually disappeared despite being disentangled. Kleenex got entangled with a tight wrap around her head, could not be disentangled, and disappeared. Punctuation was hit and killed by a ship off Cape Breton. Admiral disappeared a while after her entanglement.

Bibliography

Baker, S. S., & Palumbi, S. R., 'Which Whales Are Hunted? A Molecular Genetic Approach to Monitoring Whaling,' *Science*: Sept 9, 1994; 265:5178.

Bierce, Ambrose, *The Devil's Dictionary*, A. & C. Boni, New York, reprint 1935.

Boswell, James, *The Life of Samuel Johnson*, 1791, Viking Press, London, reprint August 1979.

Bosworth, Joseph, *An Anglo-Saxon Dictionary*, based on manuscript collections, edited and enlarged by T. Northcote Toller, Oxford University Press, Oxford, 1976.

Chamberlain, W. (attrib.), 'No Moa, No Moa, in Aotearoa,' radio, Wellington, c1960.

Ciardi, John, *I Met a Man*, illustrated by Robert Osborn, Houghton Mifflin, Boston, 1961.

Edo Right Whale, Anonymous section detail of "*Geigyo Hinshu Zukan" (Fourteen Varieties of Whales)* 1760. Image courtesy New Bedford Whaling Museum.

Eliot, T. S., 'The Love Song of J. Alfred Prufrock' and 'Preludes,' from *The Waste Land and Other Poems*, Faber & Faber, London, reprint 1972.

French, Marilyn, *The Women's Room*, Summit Books, New York, 1977.

Hubbard, Edna Elbert, *Letters of Edna St Vincent Millay*, Ed. Allen R. MacDougall, Harper and Brothers, New York and London, 1952.

Ihimaera, Witi, *The Whale Rider*, Harcourt, Auck., 1987.

Jaquet, N. *et al*, 'Track of the Research Vessel & Sperm Whale Encounters', *Sperm Whale Distribution*, Marine Ecology Progress Series, 1996, 135:1–9.

Jones, Frank Pierce, *Freedom to Change*, Mouritz, London, 1997.

Kahukiwa, Robyn, *Paikea*, Puffin Books, Auckland, 1993.

Kelly, Walt, *The Best of Pogo*, Eds. Mrs Walt Kelly and Bill Crouch Jr, Simon & Schuster, N Y,1982.

Le Guin, Ursula K. *The Left Hand of Darkness*, Harper & Row, New York, reprint 1980.

Lowell, Robert, *Selected Poems*, Farrar, Straus & Giroux, N.Y. 1973.

McCutchen, D.K., 'DDT & PCBs Found in Hector's Dolphins, Compared to Recorded Levels Across Several Species in Literature', thesis, University of Otago, 1993.

McCutchen, D.K. *Whale Winds*. IdentityTheory.com, 2007.

Melville, Herman, *Moby-Dick or The Whale: Extracts*, Oxford
University Press, London 1851, reprint 1938.

New York Zoological Society, 'Townsend Chart of Sperm Whale
Kills along The Line, 1761–1920', *Zoologica*, 1935.

Rukeyser, Muriel, *The Collected Poems*, McGraw-Hill, New
York, 1978.

Shakespeare, William, *Hamlet.*

Shakespeare, William, *The Tempest.*

JACKLEG PRESS

V. Joshua Adams, Scott Shibuya Brown, Brian Rivka Clifton, Brittney Corrigan, Jessica Cuello, Barbara Cully, Alison Cundiff, Neil de la Flor, Suzanne Frischkorn, Victoria Garza, Reginald Gibbons, Joachim Glage, Caroline Goodwin, Kathryn Kruse, Meagan Lehr, Brigitte Lewis, Jenny Magnus, D.K. McCutchen, Jean McGarry, Rita Mookerjee, Mamie Morgan, Alexis Orgera, Karen Rigby, Jo Salas, Maureen Seaton, Kristine Snodgrass, Cornelia Maude Spelman, Peter Stenson, Melissa Studdard, Curious Theatre, Gemini Wahhaj, Megan Weiler, Cassandra Whitaker, David Wesley Williams

jacklegpress.org

Printed in the USA
CPSIA information can be obtained
at www.ICGtesting.com
JSHW020247171023
50305JS00004B/137